There Are No Limits to Growth

Lyndon H. LaRouche, Jr.

There Are No Limits to Growth

Lyndon H. LaRouche, Jr.

FIRST EDITION
New Benjamin Franklin House / New York

Copyright © 1983 by Lyndon H. LaRouche, Jr.

ISBN: 0-933488-31-9

Design: Virginia Baier

AMAZON PRINT ON DEMAND EDITION
ISBN: 9781980206323
Copyright © 2018 by Lyndon H. LaRouche, Jr.
Published by EIR News Service, Inc.

All rights reserved. No part of this publication may be reproduced, stored in a retrieval system, or transmitted, in any form or by any means, electronic, mechanical, photocopying, recording, or otherwise, without the prior written permission of EIR News Service, P.O. Box 17390, Washington, D.C. 20041

TABLE OF CONTENTS

Introduction By Helga Zepp-LaRouche   vii

Author's Acknowledgments   ix

1   Mother Nature Kills German Forests   1

2   Who Was Behind Thomas Malthus?   22
      British Political Economy
      The Opium-Trafficking Families of New England

3   Bertrand Russell's Dream of World-Empire   59
      The Malthusian Logic of Nuclear Deterrence
      "The Third and Final Roman Empire"
      Religion, Culture and Malthusianism in Russia

4   The Forests and Cities of Mars   108

5   The General Law of Population   144
      What Does "Geometric Increase" Signify?
      Kepler and The Five Platonic Solids
      The Principle of Least Action

6   For Example, Britain's Positive Choice of Role   184
      Plato, St. Augustine, and Dante Alighieri
      The Required Policy--In General

What Is the Club of Life? 213
   The Founding Principles of the Club of Life
Biography of Lyndon H. LaRouche, Jr. 219

List of Tables and Figures

Table 1. Energy Flux Density 12
Table 2. Comparison of Delivered Electricity 14
Development of Earth's Population 19
Table 3. Electromagnetic Spectrum 111
Table 4. Temperature Increase Through Focusing of
Laser Beams 112
Table 5. Basic Consumption of Oxygen Water and Food Per
Week for Space Travelers 115
Table 6. Requirements for an Earth-Moon Trip 115
Figure 1. Growth in Accordance With the Fibonacci Series 154
The Golden Section 154
Figure 2. Construction of a Pentagon from a Circle 155
Figure 3. Construction of a Pentagon from a Triangle 157
Figures 4-5. Self-similar spiral on a cone 158
The Platonic Solids 162
Figure 6. Fundamental Theorem of Differential Topology 168
Figure 7. Construction from the Circle 169
Figure 8. Spiral Model of Solar System 182
Figure 9. Time Line of Human History 191
Figure 10. Producing the Four Other Solids from the
Dodecahedron 197
Figure 11. Kepler's Derivation of the Musical Intervals 202

Helga Zepp-LaRouche, Founder of the Club of Life

Introduction

by Helga Zepp-LaRouche

Founder of the Club of Life

Dear Reader,

The *Club of Life* was founded on Oct. 22, 1982 in Rome, Wiesbaden, and many other cities around the world, and today, a year later, is already an anti-Malthusian mass movement in which many leading politicians, scientists, trade unionists, industry representatives, teachers, jurists, and others collaborate on four continents and in over 30 countries.

The idea of the *Club of Life* caught fire because many people in many countries found it unbearable to see the constant spread of cultural pessimism and considered it an urgent necessity to create a new institution, based on human reason, on scientific and technological progress as well as cultural optimism.

The *Club of Rome* and its co-thinkers have in the course of over 12 years done enough mischief with their prognoses of the decline of the world à la Oswald Spengler. We can thank the Club of Rome's and similar writings, poured into the international market through a mammoth propaganda effort, for poisoning the spirit of young people in particular, who have been convinced that technological progress is the incarnation of the Devil himself.

The *Club of Life* has set for itself, among other tasks, that of proving that the theses of the *Club of Rome* are,

There Are No Limits To Growth

from a scientific standpoint, sheer quackery. This book is the first of a planned series whose goal is to discredit and counter the influence of the Club of Rome, the Aspen Institute, the World Wildlife Fund, and others. And there is no one more worthy of beginning this job than my husband, Lyndon H. LaRouche, Jr.

However, the *Club of Life* will not restrict itself in its publications to the unfortunately necessary attack on organizations which hopefully will soon be consigned by history to insignificance; rather, we want to present concrete research and development programs which demonstrate how the presently existing limits to growth can be overcome.

The *Club of Life* has set no small task for itself. We intend nothing less than to bring about a new worldwide humanist renaissance. We want to orient ourselves to earlier high points of human culture, the Classical and Renaissance periods, and study how mankind overcame the earlier dark ages which show close parallels with the present situation. We proceed with confidence that we, strengthened by the superior examples of great humanists of the past, can again bring forth great composers, poets, and scientists.

And we are firmly convinced that man is endowed with reason, and that it cannot be mankind's purpose that only a few individuals reach the level of reason in their thinking; on the contrary, we are convinced that through our efforts the Age of Reason can be attained.

May this book enrich and inspire you.

Helga Zepp-LaRouche
Wiesbaden, August 1983

Author's Acknowledgments

To list, by name and contribution, all of those whose researches have more or less directly contributed some important part to the content of this book, would require a book in itself. In place of such a detailed acknowledgment, a few general remarks and some examples are given here.

For more than a decade, this writer has served as *primus inter pares* within an international association whose functions have taken the general shape and content of Plato's Academy at Athens, or, perhaps one might say either the specifications for an Academy given by Gottfried Leibniz, or the work of constructing Academies on Leibniz's model by Dr. Benjamin Franklin. For most of that period, this association's day-to-day activities have been linked most prominently in developing and maintaining an international political-intelligence news service. It has been chiefly work done in connection with the work of that news service which produced the research reflected in the following chapters.

In form of organization, this news service was constructed according to the model of common features of the leading newsweeklies of the United States, dividing the world into regions, and nations within regions, and adding to areas of special responsibility so defined special subjects such as political economy, science, law, music, and so forth. The news service's functioning was distinguished most significantly from the work of most leading newsweeklies on two points. The editorial standpoint adopted has been that of fifteenth-century, Golden Renaissance humanism, the standpoint typified by Leibniz and, more or less efficiently, Dr. Benjamin Franklin. The method of approach to current events has been emphasis on deep historical studies of the political and intellectual history of the general populations and factions existing in each area of specialist responsibility.

The historical researches fostered by these policies of practice have had two notable points of emphasis in common, apart from the governing, specified humanist standpoint. First, the research done has emphasized primary historical sources, collecting as comprehensively representative a selection of works as possible written by spokesmen of leading factions during the period being examined. Second, emphasis on uncovering the efficient continuity of evolving development of cultural values and internal history of ideas over successive intervals of the past, into the present.

This attention to primary sources, comprehensive selections of correspondence and other writings from the period being considered, has demonstrated most frequently that the account of history provided by most university textbooks and similar published sources today is chiefly mythology. In most current history textbooks and related sources, a small selection of dates, names of political factions, of key personalities, and so forth, is assembled, and these facts rearranged in such a way as to fit some academically accepted explanation. The fraudulent accounts of U.S. history by such influential writers as Frederick Jackson Turner, Charles A. Beard, Walter Lippmann, and Arthur Schlesinger, Jr., are unfortunately not untypical of the versions of national histories offered by academics of leading universities in most nations. What such textbooks offer would be unrecognizable to the leading figures actually engaged in the momentous struggles of the places and periods indicated.

Although the popularized mythologies about the past

Author's Acknowledgments

generally accepted today may, and usually do, shape general thinking about the past--and present--history has a remarkably efficient habit of circumventing the efforts of those who attempt to rewrite it. As it is the past which has created the institutions and ideas transmitted into the present, the real past unconsciously influences the behavior of peoples and nations in ways and to a degree which most present populations, even history professors as well as governments, too rarely suspect. What you do today, may be determined in significant degree by a great event which your history professor insists never existed.

There is something even more important to be learned from real history. History is properly examined as a scientific study of the way in which the policy decisions adopted by one generation shape the consequences striking powerfully upon their posterity one, two, three, or more generations distant. There are, as the historian Friedrich Schiller proposed for the study of universal history, discernible laws governing the process of unfolding of history. These laws, which can be discovered only by rigorous study of internal intellectual history of mankind in each period over long expanses of time, are the key to the future. The outcome of what we choose today, over the span of several future generations--say a hundred years or so into the future--can be predetermined to a significant degree. We can not predetermine what our successors will decide to do, of course; but we do predetermine the general conditions in which the next generations will find the world, or our nation in particular, and we do influence changes in culture which will strongly affect their choices in decision-making even two or three or more generations ahead.

In addition to such general matters concerning longer sweeps of history, our brief mortal lives are so much with us, and the immediate problems of this year, the preceding year, and the next, so fiercely grip our attentions, that we tend to exaggerate the authority of that aspect of knowledge we call "experience." In particular, we tend to assume that experience teaches how others will respond to our choices in behavior, or teaches us what will succeed and what will fail, more generally. Then, abruptly, especially under conditions of crisis, events take a turn which violates every bit of what we imagine we have learned from experience. Suddenly, it appears to us that the world has gone mad, resembling a condition in which the solar system might have changed suddenly the laws governing the orbits of its planets and moons.

If we know history in terms of primary sources, we recognize that there was nothing unlawful, unpredictable in such sudden changes in behavior of peoples and nations. The same abruptness of changes in institutions and general behavior has occurred often before, and has always occurred in a manner which permits lawful interpretation. Ordinary day-to-day experience, even over a span of several generations, is not a competent array of empirical evidence from which to adduce the actual, deeper laws of human behavior. To understand breaking developments in a European-culture-dominated world of today, it is more or less indispensable to know the internal history of that European culture over a span of approximately 2,500 years. That is not long enough, perhaps, but if we know all of the important periods of European history since Solon of Athens, if we know each crucial period more or less intimately in terms of the circumstances and ideas of that period, and also know how the circumstances and ideas of one period are linked efficiently to its past, we have the foundations in knowledge to begin to understand what is actually occurring in breaking developments in the world today.

That view of universal history used to be the standpoint

Author's Acknowledgments

of reference for policies of providing a general classical education to the young, up through approximately the ages of between sixteen and eighteen years. We began the education of the youth in history with study of Greek and Latin classics, not to the purpose that he or she should speak classical Greek, but that the youth might have the foundations for tracing the subsequent history of institutions and ideas from a well-defined initial point of reference, approximately 2,500 years ago. This was intended to be the general development of the potentialities of the mind of the future citizen of a republic, a citizen qualified to judge properly the practical consequences of adopting or refusing to adopt a certain national policy, or even a personal course in life.

Since this adopted approach to history by the news service early proved fruitful, aiding evaluations which proved superior in usefulness to those afforded from other sources, the emphasis on the historical method was increased greatly. Here, those accumulated resources are applied to three questions: (1) Where did Malthusianism come from, how, and why? (2) What would be the consequences of failing to crush the Malthusian policy-impulse now? (3) How is that Malthusian policy-impulse to be defeated?

Since the facts concerning the history of Malthusianism may have been previously unknown to many readers, we note the scope of some of the investigations whose contributions made the corresponding content of this present book possible.

Into 1978, a team of more than two-score researchers conducted an in-depth research into the history of the international narcotics traffic, with great assistance from the archives of U.S. federal intelligence and enforcement agencies. This inquiry overlapped massive work done by teams assisting Mrs. Carol White in preparing her 1980 book, *The New Dark Ages Conspiracy*, and the author and David P. Goldman in preparing the historical study of the development of British political economy published in 1980 as *The Ugly Truth About Milton Friedman*. The principal work done on the history of the New England drug-trafficking families and their connection to the Aaron Burr plots was assembled by Anton Chaitkin for his *Treason in America* series, drawing upon the work of more than a score of others engaged in overlapping areas. The primary work on American history was done by teams working in collaboration with Nancy Spannaus, Christopher White, Allen Salisbury, and Robert Zubrin's study of the racialists of the American Museum of Natural History.

The work on the Greek classical period was developed under the direction of Criton Zoakos and Dr. Uwe Parpart, and Zoakos also did much of the work on Byzantium and Venice. From the Italian side, work on Venice and the European black nobility's history involves work done in Italy, Germany, France, the United States, and elsewhere, by persons too numerous to be listed here. The work on economic science is predominantly this writer's own, but not without debts to historical re- searches on this matter by about two-score others. On matters of physics per se, the obligations are chiefly to the Fusion Energy Foundation and its European and Ibero-American affiliates. On the internal history of science, the debt is to teams coordinated by Dr. Parpart and the work coordinated by a gifted mathematician, Dr. Jonathan Tennenbaum. On the Golden Renaissance, and on the German classical period, the author's debt is most directly--to his wife and collaborator, Helga Zepp-LaRouche, but also to the numerous persons working closely with her in their original researches on these subjects.

In total, several hundred persons have contributed

Author's Acknowledgments

original research directly or indirectly reflected in the following pages. Those unnamed will recognize their contribution as implicitly acknowledged, and will agree with the service to which their efforts have been directed in this way.

Lyndon Hermyle LaRouche, Jr.

Wiesbaden, Federal Republic of Germany

June 1983

There Are No Limits to Growth

Eruption of the submarine volcano Surtur in November 1963.

1

Mother Nature Kills German Forests

Between March 28 and April 4, 1982, El Chichón, in the Mexican Yucatan peninsula, rumbled, steamed, and exploded, putting an estimated 3 to 4 cubic kilometers of material into the Earth's atmosphere. This act of massive pollution by Mother Nature included an estimated 15 million tons of sulfur and its compounds, 15 percent of the total of the world's industry in a year.

What goes up, usually comes down. The pollution put into the Earth's upper atmosphere by El Chichén gradually settled down, sometimes falling back to Earth as polluted rain. In Germany, the clamor erupted: "The forests are dying! We must save the forests!"

As a matter of pagan beliefs, many Germans insisted that it was industry which was responsible for the death of the forests. To such fanatics, the culprit must be industry, whether the charge was true or not. What about the pollution from El Chichón? Facts mean nothing to today's so-called "ecologists," especially when the facts prove that it is Mother Nature herself who is the culprit.

There was another fact which the pagans of Germany overlooked in their zeal to reduce employment among Germany's trade union members. Even forests, like babies, must be fed or they may die. Forests require, generally, a minimum rainfall of 90 centimeters per year; the dying portions of the German forests were not dying of lack of rainfall. Forests must not only drink; they must be fed.

Decade after decade, cut trees are harvested from the

forests and hauled off to the lumber mill or the paper mill. In each tree carried away, there are some of the essential chemical compounds the tree has taken from the soil, chemical compounds without which future trees can not grow properly, or, ultimately, even grow at all. It is the same as with the farmer's need to put chemical fertilizers and essential trace-elements back into his soil, if he expects to have healthy crops in the future.

Suppose we do not feed the forests from which timber is being harvested decade after decade? Eventually, the forest will die of hunger. Also, like any undernourished human being, or other living organism, undernourished trees are more vulnerable to diseases and poisons than well-fed trees. The German forests are not suffering from too much chemical output of industry, but from too little: too little chemical nourishment of the sort needed to maintain the soil in the condition for growing healthy trees.

The classical case of destruction of a forest in recent times is the cutting of vast tracts of the Brazilian rain forest. Some of the cutting was done to clear areas for labor-intensive farming. Some was cut to produce charcoal for making steel. In both cases, the cutting was imposed upon Brazil chiefly by outside pressures. The labor-intensive agriculture projects were based on the philosophy of the World Bank and Brandt Commission, the so-called "appropriate technologies" dogma, which argues that countries below the Tropic of Cancer should not use modern agronomy, modern industry, but only "appropriate," labor-intensive agriculture, and small, primitive, local industries. The use of charcoal for making steel goes back to sixteenth-century Europe; it was proposed to Brazil as a way of saving on foreign imports of petroleum and coal, and as a way of not investing in developing Brazil's own nuclear and fossil fuel potentialities.

The result of these "appropriate technologies" practices was a disaster, potentially a global ecological disaster.

The heavy rains of a rain forest area wash out the chemicals from the soil year after year. As a result, nearly all of the chemicals essential for plant life in such forests are stored in the trees themselves. The classic case of ignoring this fact is the collapse of the ancient culture of Angkor Wat in Kampuchea. If trees are removed, and slash-and-burn methods of "appropriate technology" are used to clear the rain forest area for primitive, labor-intensive methods of agriculture, the soil very soon turns into a rock-like substance called laterite, a poor grade of aluminum ore. Agriculture collapses after a few years of such "appropriate technology," a fact repeated quickly in the case of Brazil.

Giant rain forests have another ecological function. They exert a great degree of control over the world's weather. The moisture sent into the atmosphere by trees forms a rising column, a column of warm moisture rising into the stratosphere, which is an essential part of maintaining a large, permanent high-pressure area. Destroy a large part of such a forest, and the world's weather will change, as cutting of the Brazilian rain forest caused such a change.

This effect is not limited to rain forests. Pressures by international financial agencies pushed some nations of the African Sahel region to intensify taxation of parts of their populations engaged in grazing of herds. To pay the taxes, the grazing was increased. Overgrazing destroyed the barrier between the semi-arid Sahel and the deserts; the cessation of moisture-flows into the atmosphere because of this, was sufficient to cause a shift in weather patterns in northern Africa, interacting with effects of a shift of the Amazon High. Semi-arid regions of the Sahel were transformed into a creeping desert. With industrial modes of water-management and related technologies, this desertification of the Sahel region can be reversed.

In India, a lack of industrial fuels for households pushed rural populations into stripping large regions, including the Himalayan foothills, of trees and brush. Forests not only maintain watersheds, essential for regulating stable brooks, and rivers, as well as underground water levels. Forests consume a relatively large percentile of the sunlight falling upon the area, turning the sunlight into biomass, and moderating the temperature of the adjoining area. India's water problems increased, and entire regions once comfortable during the hot season of the year have risen in average temperature, to become unbearably hot.

It is not the growth of industry which destroys the world's forests. In most cases, the cause is a lack of industrial output, a lack of good industrial management of the ecosphere. Over the past fifteen years, the greatest single cause for destruction of the world's "ecology" has been the toleration of the policies demanded by the so-called "ecologists," the so-called "neo-Malthusians" of the Club of Rome, of the International Institute for Applied Systems Analysis (IIASA), of the World Wildlife Fund, the Aspen Institute, the Ford Foundation, the Rockefeller Foundation, the U.S. Sierra Club, and so forth and so on. We are not putting enough industrially-produced energy, in the form of water management, chemicals, and so forth, into the farming of the Earth's biosphere. At the same time, we are using biomass for fuel and other "traditional" uses, in cases we should be using nuclear-generated energy supplies, and using modern, industrially produced materials in place of timber for housing and so forth.

Meanwhile, at the opposite extreme, since approximately the 1920s in Germany, some of us have been planning mankind's exploration and colonization of space. During the 1950s and 1960s, well-designed plans for human colonization of the Moon and Mars began to be developed. With development and use of controlled thermonuclear fusion, frequent travel between Mars and a large, orbiting space-station parked near the Earth would become practicable. With thermonuclear fusion energy and use of directed-beam technologies, including high-powered lasers, we will have the basic repertoire of technologies needed to create and maintain "artificial Earth-like" environments on the Moon or Mars, probably beginning with the use of Earth's natural orbiting-satellite space-station, the Moon, as a logistical base in nearby space, from which to launch the long leg of exploration of nearby and deep space.

Can mankind construct a forest on Mars? If we resume the rates of technological progress we may remember from the pre-1967 period of research and development efforts of the U.S.A.'s National Aeronautics and Space Administration (NASA), we will be able to do just that during the twenty-first century. With thermonuclear fusion technologies we shall possess cheaply-produced, abundant energy supplies in the needed quantities at the best cost required to develop the necessary artificial, Earth-like environments under "plastic bubbles." With directed-beam technologies, such as high-powered lasers and coherent particle-beams, and with related classes of technology of relativistic physics, the productive power of an average human individual will zoom to between ten and a hundred times that on Earth today. With aid of progress in biotechnology, we shall be able to engineer properties into trees and other plants to produce types suited to the conditions of artificial, Earth-like environments.

If this is possible during a period less than a century ahead, why can we not solve the much less challenging problems of improving the ecology on Earth today? With the combinations of very high energy-flux density thermonuclear fusion, directed-beam and related technologies, and biotechnology, we can manufacture air, water, and so forth where they do not exist today in space, and can provide plant life the properties needed to cope with special problems; perhaps we might even develop a new, improved version of chlorophyll, to double or treble the energy-gathering powers of the plant life. Today, we either have such technologies, or are at the edge of mastering them. Why, then, do we continue to tolerate conditions on Earth which even existing technologies are proven capable of solving?

The reason for these miserable conditions is a simple reason. Some people, people with a great deal of power over the periodicals, universities, financial institutions, and political parties of much of the world, simply do not wish society to solve these problems.

Take the case of a fellow known as Rudolf Bahro. This fellow once enjoyed an international reputation as a great fighter for freedom and human welfare generally, at the point he was in the process of leaving East Germany (the German Democratic Republic) for sanctuary in the West. Now, many of us suspect that the East German government was delighted to see its competitor, West Germany, enjoy the benefits of Herr Bahro's advice. In mid-March, 1983, Herr Bahro presented an audience some seeds held in his hand--presumably seeds of grain--and declared that these seeds represented the beginning of the evils which afflict man today.

Some very basic facts about the economic history and prehistory of human life on earth show exactly what Herr Bahro was implicitly proposing.

The lowest form of human life known is what is called a "hunting and gathering society," the kind of society to which mankind would presumably return if Herr Bahro's demands were accepted. In such a form of society, an area of between ten and fifteen square kilometers of the habitable surface of the Earth is required to sustain an average individual. This means a total human population of the Earth of never more than approximately ten millions individuals. This fact prompts us to ask Herr Bahro to list, by name, the approximately four and a half billions individuals presently living on Earth, whom he proposes to kill, in order to reduce the population levels down to those possible without the "agricultural revolution" which occurred most probably ten to twelve thousand years ago?

Not only is such a pre-agricultural-revolution form of society a very thinly-populated society. The prevailing life expectancy is significantly less than twenty years of age, and the life of each local tribe as a whole is extremely precarious. Although Herr Bahro has not stated that he proposes to boycott the food and fiber produced by the agricultural revolution, he seems otherwise sincere in asserting that he considers it a mistake ever to have left the spiritually invigorating cultural climate of the extinct South African strandlooper, pelting to death washed up, dying fish and whatnot which the surf has cast upon the beach.

Admittedly, Herr Bahro's views are presently those of an extremely eccentric, although organized and growing, tiny minority. Nonetheless, his views are only the most extreme version of the broader spectrum of neo-Malthusian dogmatists generally. So-called "environmentalists" or "ecologists" infest increasingly large portions of most major political parties, as well as the variously neo-Nazi-led and "leftist." varieties of "anti-technology" sects. Moreover, most of the major news media, the major entertainment media, the courts, legislatures, and powerful, very wealthy foundations, are more or less saturated with neo-Malthusian policies and pro-Club of Rome propaganda.

There Are No Limits to Growth

During recent years, it has been overlooked, how recent the mass-based "ecologist" movements are. The first movements were organized, top-down at the end of 1969, pulling together remnants of the 1950s Ban the Bomb movements, the 1965-1969 anti-Vietnam War movements, and the New Left generally, on both sides of the Atlantic. "Sun Day," during spring 1970, was the first of the demonstrations organized top-down by governmental agencies and private foundations for the "ecologist causes." The banning of the pesticide DDT, (on fraudulent pretexts), and the campaign against nuclear energy came only slightly later. The spread of this ideology is little more than ten years old.

The present-day neo-Malthusian organizing did not really get under way outside the ranks of the "re-programmed leftists" until 1972, with the publication of a book called *Limits to Growth*. This book's production was sponsored by the Club of Rome, and its publication as used to launch the public relations campaign which made the Club of Rome almost-an instant major policy-influencing institution.

The *Limits to Growth* was based on a computer-assisted study conducted under the direction of two professors from the Massachusetts Institute of Technology (U.S.A.), Dennis Meadows and Jay Forrester. The study itself was most conspicuously fraudulent on two leading counts. First, in attempting to prove that industrial society was using up its remaining natural resources very rapidly, Meadows and Forrester greatly understated the known quantities of such resources. Second, more important, Meadows and Forrester projected the rate of consumption of natural resources by using systems of simultaneous linear equations. The very use of such linear equations for a computer "model" of that sort, builds into the computer projections the assumption that absolutely no technological

Mother Nature Kills German Forests

progress is occurring in society. In fact, technological progress, including fundamental redefinitions of what "natural resources" means, has been the outstanding feature of European civilization for five hundred years. *The Limits to Growth* depended upon the assumption that such technological progress had come to a sudden, absolute stop.

How could anyone have believed such nonsense? Every qualified scientist knew that the kinds of arguments used by the Club of Rome were a fraud. Most engineers knew it. Industrial corporations knew it. If the news media checked with scientists, they, too, would have known it. If governments and political parties had behaved responsibly, they would have denounced the Club of Rome and its *Limits of Growth* as a monstrous hoax.

If we are running out of coal, and we do have about 200 years known supply at present rates of consumption, why not use more abundant nuclear energy, and why not concentrate on speeding up development of almost unlimited resources of thermonuclear fusion? We are not running out of petroleum either; we are discovering vast new petroleum fields faster than we use up the old fields. However, if we are worried about carbon dioxide build-ups and other pollution caused by fossil fuel combustion, why not shift at an accelerating rate into nuclear and thermonuclear generation of process-heat?

"Radioactivity"? Nonsense! A nuclear energy plant radiates less radioactive waste into the environment than a coal-fired plant generating the same number of kilowatt-hours. A nuclear plant radiates less radioactivity into the environment than a brick wall. A person leaning against a nuclear plant receives less radioactivity than while traveling in a transatlantic jet, or a weekend's ski trip in the U.S. Rocky Mountains or Swiss Alps. If one is concerned about such levels of radioactivity, one ought to insist that never more than two (naturally slightly radioactive) human bodies ought to be allowed in the same bed.

"Nuclear plant accidents"? The "lesson of Three Mile Island" in Pennsylvania is, first, that the combination of circumstances involved could occur only through sabotage, and, second, that the "accident" proved totally the perfection of the safety precautions built into nuclear plants today. The tales of the "China Syndrome" and other Grimm stories issued by the news media were all a deliberate hoax, a lie, as every investigation of the matter proved during and after the "accident."

To cause a nuclear accident, either one would have to drop a nuclear bomb directly onto the plant, or carry in and place the most sophisticated combination of shaped charges imaginable. In any case, the mass of steel and concrete built into such plants make them the most bomb-proof structures presently in existence in the world. If we employ nuclear fuels of the thorium-cycle, for example, even the infinitesimal possibilities for some degree of nuclear accident become approximately absolute zero.

All this is well-known, even by the scientifically-trained liars trotted out as "authorities" by the anti-nuclear propagandists.

In the case of thermonuclear fusion, the possibility of nuclear accidents is automatically absolutely zero. The components of a thermonuclear reaction, such as those used in hydrogen bombs, are either a combination of lithium and an isotope of hydrogen, deuterium, or deuterium and tritium, the latter another isotope of hydrogen, or deuterium and deuterium. The latter two combinations produce so-called "clean explosions," without primary radioactive fall-out. To cause a thermonuclear ignition requires temperature equivalents in the order of between 5×10^7 and 5×10^8 degrees Kelvin, and even then, the ignition will not occur without the proper physical principles of precise

Mother Nature Kills German Forests

hydrodynamic self-focussing of the material, to effect what is called *isentropic compression*. Any disruption, such as an accident or being hit directly by a 10 megaton bomb, means that the plant's thermonuclear reaction stops abruptly.

Thermonuclear fusion is far superior to nuclear fission, but we require large-scale use of nuclear fission to supply the energy needed to develop a thermonuclear fusion-based economy. Some figures are helpful in making the point.

In the statistical theory of heat, today, we measure the level of heat processes in units we call *energy-flux density*. This measures the number of kilowatt-hours passing through an area of cross-section of the heat-generating process. The following two tables, compiled in 1979, show the comparative energy-flux densities of various sources of energy, and also the comparative costs of electrical energy produced using such sources.

There Are No Limits to Growth

Table 1: Energy-Flux Density

Energy Source	Density In Kilowatts/Square Meter
Solar—Biomass	0.0001
Solar—Earth surface	0.2
Solar—near-Sun orbit (5 millions miles)	1.4
Fossil Fuels	10,000.00
Solar—at Sun's surface	20,000.00
Fission	70,000.00
Fusion (first commercial types)	70,000.00
Fusion (next century)	$10^{15}+$

Table 2: Comparison of Delivered Electrical Power
(in U.S.A. dollars)

	Total Energy Costs (mils/kw-hr)	Total Energy Prices (mils/kw-hr)	Capital Invested ($ billions)
Oil	25.1	45.7	$ 0.94
Coal	24.2	31.7	0.97
Coal Gas	41.7	55.7	1.67
Light Water Nuclear	27.8	28.5	1.16
Fast Breeder	33.7	33.9	1.43
Fusion (early types)	45.2	45.2	1.92
Solar Collector	490.0	490.0	20.90
Solar Cells	680.0	680.0	28.90

(Source: Fusion Energy Foundation, U.S.A.)

The simplest of the physical principles involved in choosing among energy sources is that the higher the level of energy-flux density, the more efficient the energy source is. Not only is less heat wasted, but the higher the energy-flux density, the greater the potential of the process-heat to accomplish work.

Mother Nature Kills German Forests

To appreciate the importance of this, including the important question of maintaining forests, we must consider another important kind of figure. This figure has a name which may appear frightening to the layman at first glance; we shall show that it is easily understood. This datum is named *potential relative population-density*. We explain the meaning of this figure, and then show its relationship to the business of maintaining forests.

Given a population inhabiting a certain territory, and let that territory be measured in square-kilometers of habitable area. By developing and using the natural resources available in that area, how many people can be maintained through the work of the population's labor force? On the average, the answer is given as the average number of persons per average square-kilometer. Persons per square-kilometer is *population-density*.

That figure is not an adequate measurement. Land varies in quality, so that one square-kilometer is not of the same quality for human habitation as another square-kilometer. Those desirable qualities of land, which express such differences, are variable qualities. Man may improve the land, or deplete it. The quality of land is the net result of combined depletions and improvements of its qualities. Therefore, we say that the value of all square-kilometers are not the same; they are different, and they are variable. Therefore, we must measure population-density in terms of relative qualities of the land inhabited: *relative population-density*.

The present level of population is not necessarily a measurement of what the population level could be. We must determine what that population could become, as a maximum, given the kinds of production technologies presently in use. What is the potential level of population, given those technologies? That is the general meaning of *potential relative population-density*.

There Are No Limits to Growth

Development of the Earth's Population
(to 1920, from United Nations' Statistical Yearbook, figures in millions)

	1650	1750	1800	1850	1900	1920	1940	1950	1960	1980	2000
Europe and U.S.S.R.	103	144	193	274	423	487	575	573	639	791	973
Asia (not including U.S.S.R.)	257	437	595	656	857	966	1244	1381	1651	2557	4401
North America	1	1	6	26	81	117	144	166	199	272	388
Central and South America	7	10	23	33	63	91	130	163	212	387	756
Africa	100	100	100	100	141	141	191	222	273	458	860
Oceania and Australia	2	2	2	2	6	9	11	13	16	22	32
Earth	470	694	919	1091	1571	1811	2295	2517	2990	4487	7410

At the first stage of human development, that of hunting and gathering, at most one human being per square kilometer could be supported under ideal conditions, so that no more than approximately 10 million human beings could survive on earth. The transition to animal husbandry and nomadic pastoral economy increased population density to around 8 human beings per square kilometer; agriculture in its primitive form brought the level to approximately 20 human beings per square kilometer.

Industrial society brought tremendous progress. Modern energy-intensive agriculture increased population density to around 100 human beings per square kilometer. The relative potential population density of the earth thus increased to some 10 billion human beings.

Mother Nature Kills German Forests

We have already indicated that the potential relative population-density of primitive society is about 0.06 to 0.10/square-kilometer: about 10 millions maximum population. There exist today approximately 4.5 billions individuals, more than 100 times the levels of primitive man. Since a factor of "10" is called *one order of magnitude*, this means that mankind has raised its potential relative population-density by two orders of magnitude. With full use of existing levels of technology, combined with the thermonuclear, directed-beam, and bio-technology coming into existence now, our planet could sustain a population of tens of billions of persons, and at an average standard of living higher than that for the United States during the early 1970s: a rise above primitive society by *three orders of magnitude*!

No beast, or any other lower form of life could *willfully* increase in potential relative population-density by even one order of magnitude. Man is fundamentally different from the beasts. Man is not merely a creature of instinctive potentialities, a mere creature of animal-like perceptions of pleasure and pain. Man is somehow very different. Man has the potential of Reason, the power to make creative discoveries which advance his scientific knowledge, and to convert such scientific advances into advances in technology. We are able to uncover, with increasing perfection, the lawful, universal principles which order universal creation, and to master nature with increasing power, through guiding ourselves to change our ways of behavior in accordance with universal laws.

The successive technological advances accumulated by human culture since the level of Herr Bahro's utopia, have increased man's potential relative population-density by between two and three orders of magnitude.

This technological progress, this increase in human potential, has been accomplished by an increasing

There Are No Limits to Growth

command over energy. Beginning with the agricultural revolution, and ocean fishing in boats earlier, mankind has increased the amount of useful energy available to the average individual, and has increased the number of kilowatt-hours' value of the amount of usable energy obtained by society per square-kilometer. Today, we can roughly measure the fertility of agricultural land by the amount of "artificial energy" used per hectare by the farmer: chemical energy of fertilizers, trace-element additions, pesticides, and electrical and other industrially-produced energy forms used for irrigation, powered machinery, and so forth. Similarly, in industry and transportation, the productive powers of the average member of the labor force are measured in first approximation by the amount of industrially-produced energy used per capita.

This technological progress is not merely an available option. The authors of the *Limits to Growth* are right on one point, although perhaps this was an unintentional feature of their book. If, at any point, we halt technological progress, the society foolish enough to do such a thing condemns itself to die.

Any level of productive technology requires a certain array of *raw materials* produced by agriculture, fishing, forestry, mining, and so forth. This is what we work up from the Earth around us into primary materials of production and other consumption. For any level of technology and human consumption, the amount of each such kind of raw material approximates an average requirement per capita.

The production of such primary materials therefore requires some definite percentile of the entire labor force of the society. Only the remainder of the labor force, after deducting this percentile, is available for other forms of labor. As a society uses up some of the richest and most

Mother Nature Kills German Forests

accessible natural sources of raw materials-production, the amount of labor a society must expend to produce a constant per capita amount of raw materials rises. This rise in cost lowers the productivity of labor on the average. Fewer individuals can be sustained, on the average, by the output produced by an average member of the labor force. In other words, the potential relative population-density falls. If the technology of production remains constant, the rise in costs caused by depletion of critical kinds of natural resources is a rise which continues without limit. Therefore, for this reason, the potential relative population-density would fall without limit under those conditions.

At the point the society's potential relative population-density falls below the population-density of the existing population, the Four Horsemen of the Apocalypse enter. Famine promotes desperate strife. War and bloody civil commotions worsen the conditions of famine. The famine-stricken population becomes a breeder of diseases, spiraling into epidemics and pandemics, as was the case during the early fourteenth century Europe. The breakdown of agriculture and hygienic institutions promotes the eruptions of pestilences. The society is conquered, collapses, or changes its ways abruptly.

Technological progress prevents such catastrophes in two related ways. First, simply by increasing the productive powers of labor, technological progress overcomes the rising costs of production of essential raw materials. Second, technological revolutions redefine the range of usable natural resources, and introduce new kinds of raw materials to the bill of requirements, Just as the industrial revolution's use of coal overcame the threatened collapse of Europe caused by exhaustion of forests.

Technological Progress is indispensable even to maintain a constant level of potential relative population-density. Therefore, constantly rising levels of energy

There Are No Limits to Growth

supplies, both per square-kilometer and per capita are indispensable to the survival of society. These growing energy supplies must become relatively cheaper: The cost of producing the average amount of increased energy per capita must tend to be significantly less than the old cost of producing less energy per capita. The energy-flux density of energy supplies must also increase, at least in a general way. There must also be periodic revolutions in the definition of the term "natural resources," even under conditions of a constant potential relative population-density.

In connection with matters of agriculture and forestry, there exists today the widespread, but false opinion that the fertility of the soil for agriculture lies essentially with an assumedly natural fertility of land. This was, more or less exactly, the argument submitted by the radically feudalist faction of eighteenth-century France, the so-called Physiocrats. The history of agriculture in the United States, since it began during the seventeenth century, is perhaps the best case with aid of which to demonstrate the absurdity of the Physiocratic opinion. Notable, of course, is the case of California's Imperial Valley, today the most valuable agricultural land on Earth, which was, but a few decades ago, a desert. This case is exceptional in degree, but not in matters of principle. Virtually the entirety of the richness of agriculture in the United States and the earlier settlements was created out of an infertile, stubborn wilderness by means of processes of man-imposed improvements in land, improvements analogous to the investment and improvement of industrial capital. In Europe, where a longer occupation of the land by agriculture is the case, the same demonstration is immediately clear to all who know agriculture, but is less dramatically demonstrated than in the relatively brief history of agriculture in the United States.

Otherwise, one of the clearest demonstrations of the

Mother Nature Kills German Forests

same principle is the case of the forests of Germany, which are, with the rarest exceptions, man-made creations, not natural occurrences. They are not forests, but better described as tree-farms, a point immediately clear to any visitor to those pleasant parks (called forests) who has firsthand recollections of struggling through a primitive jungle or temperate zone forest. Yet, these "artificial" German forests are not to be despised because they are not "natural," any more than one would despise the produce of agriculture on our tables, on grounds that the tropical melons are not poisonous, like the ancestors of our melons in their "natural" occurrence. These "artificial forests" are better than those naturally occurring, on many important points; if they are not, it is because the tree-farmer is not meeting his responsibilities as a farmer. To the point, a good forest must be weeded, like a farmer's field, to the effect of producing a healthier forest than would occur "naturally."

A forest, like agriculture generally, is a biological system. All biological systems, except dying ones, are characterized by a property called *negentropy*. Over successful cycles of their growth, they embody greater energy than earlier, and such systems are ranked by the equivalent of energy-flux density per unit of mass-weight. Their potentialities of growth, of quality of growth, and powers of resistance to various injuries, vary with the nourishment provided by their environment. Above all, they require relatively abundant energy, energy organized in those forms they can assimilate it.

A striking illustration of the point was accomplished in Wales, Britain, by experimenters working with flax plants. It was demonstrated repeatedly, that by affording young flax plants the proper environment of temperature and nourishment, a change occurred in these plants. This change proved to be fully hereditable, although no genetic change had occurred. This heredity persisted in daughter, granddaughter, and great-granddaughter, and so forth, plants, even though those later generations had been reproduced under normal conditions, without the special conditions of temperature and nourishment employed to produce the original change.

Otherwise, in cases in which no environment-directed hereditable change occurs in plants, superior strains of plants usually require enhanced environments, especially nutrition. This enhancement takes the included forms of water-management and soil- treatment, and sometimes "hothouse" preparation of the seedlings before transplanting. All of this requires industrially-produced "artificial energy," and all of this translates into increased supplies of such "artificial energy" per hectare, whether for forest or farm. In Germany, therefore, one of the best friends of the field and forest is, traditionally, the BASF chemical plant.

It is most helpful to think about developing a forest under an artificial, bubble-covered, Earth-like environment on Mars. It is the proper point of view for thinking about problems of maintaining and improving the environment on Earth. Forcing ourselves to solve the problems associated with growing a forest on Mars, has the added benefit of forcing us to develop techniques which will be of considerable benefit to maintaining the forests on Earth.

On Mars or Earth, we require the benefits of technological progress for such undertakings. We require not only new technology for treating problems of the biosphere. We require the energy supplies such work implies. It is also indispensable that we cheapen the social cost of doing such work, through increasing the productive powers of society.

In general principles, this is not new. The principles have been known to Europe, in particular, for centuries.

Mother Nature Kills German Forests

We must ask how" and why people and institutions of considerable prestige, wealth, and influence, would have produced a doctrine as dangerously absurd as the neo-Malthusianism of the Club of Rome?

2

Who Was Behind Thomas Malthus?

In this preceding chapter, we reported that the Club of Rome's supposed "scientific work," the *Limits to Growth*, was a hoax. The data on resources used for the book was vastly inaccurate in crucial categories. The method of computer calculations was based on the astonishing assumption that all technological progress was suddenly and continuously stopped over a period of more than thirty years. The authors, and at least numerous of their leading backers, knew that the book, *Limits to Growth*, was fraudulent. Yet, during the 1970s, the Club of Rome, and most other leading "neo-Malthusians" based their campaigns more or less strictly upon the conclusions of that fraudulent book.

What was their true motive for pushing a Malthusian doctrine in which even they did not believe?

This writer and his associates have conducted thorough research, for longer than a decade, into the leading figures behind the international "neo-Malthusian" movements and projects. They have come to know representative creators and leaders of the Club of Rome, and allied organizations, and have listened to such persons describe in their own words, their true motives for creating the present-day neo-Malthusian hoax.

There is the case of Dr. Alexander King, a Paris-based British subject, formerly Director of the OECD organization adjunct to NATO, and a principal behind-the-scenes architect of the creation of the Club of Rome. Dr.

Who Was Behind Thomas Malthus?

King volunteered, in a published interview, that his true motives for sponsoring neo-Malthusian propaganda have been racialist. He insisted that the Anglo-Saxon racial stock was becoming dangerously outnumbered on this planet, and that therefore, neo-Malthusian propaganda and programs must be employed to reduce substantially the populations of darker-skinned "races." Among "darker races," King included, with some vehemence, "the Mediterranean race," a term usually understood to signify Arab, Turk, Greek, Italian, and Spaniard.

There is the case of Britain's Lord Solly Zuckerman, South African by pedigree. This high-ranking British official, who insists that he is more important than Dr. King in the creation of the Club of Rome, is currently serving as head of an Anglo-Soviet Malthusian association, the International Institute for Applied Systems Analysis (IIASA), an association cofounded with backing of the U.S.A.'s McGeorge Bundy, a Bundy described by Harvard University's famous John Kenneth Galbraith, as "head of the [U.S.] Establishment." Lord Zuckerman's views are reasonably described as dangerously savage, and his power most extensive.

In the case of leading U.S. backers of neo-Malthusian projects, there is the case of General William Draper, associated with the New York investment house of Dillon, Read. This Draper was a vocal participant in a 1932 meeting of the trustees of New York City's American Museum of Natural History. At this meeting, those assembled praised Adolf Hitler's imminent rise to power in Germany, Draper leading in special praise for the Nazis' "racial hygiene" doctrines. His Draper Fund, which backs the Population Crisis Committee, is explicitly dedicated to promoting savage population reduction of those peoples of Africa and elsewhere which Anglo-Saxon racialist fanatics view as "inferior races."

There Are No Limits to Growth

The case of Draper is not exceptional among circles associated with the American Museum of Natural History. This institution was established during the last quarter of the nineteenth century, to promote the doctrines of Charles Darwin and Thomas Huxley, which those circles have consistently understood over the intervening hundred years to mean a fight to reduce the population levels of non-Anglo-Saxon "racial stocks." During this century, the famous families of Morgan and Harriman have been most prominent in this institution; since World War I, the Harriman family has been the chief promoter of Nazi-like racialist doctrines in the name of genetics within the United States. It was not properly surprising that these families played a dominant role in putting Hjalmar Schacht's protégé, Adolf Hitler, into power in Germany, expressing special delight in Hitler's racial doctrines. These were the families, especially the Harriman family, which pushed through a 1920s immigration law in the United States, designed to stop significant immigration of such "darker-skinned races as the Mediterranean" into the United States, stipulating an annual quota to this effect.

During the late 1930s, there was a clamor in the United States for lifting the quotas against immigration of Jews threatened by Adolf Hitler's rampages. The Harrimans mobilized to prevent such special arrangements. One boatload of Jews fleeing Hitler was turned back from the United States, many returning, rejected by Harrimanite racialism, to their doom. Of the three millions or more who might have been saved from Hitler's racial persecutions, had the United States exerted leadership to this purpose, only a relative handful escaped. The Harrimans, including today's former Governor W. Averell Harriman, were enthusiastic supporters of the Italian fascist, Benito Mussolini, from the late 1920s into approximately 1938, and many among the Morgan circles continued to back Hitler into a similar late date. It was only after 1938, that

Who Was Behind Thomas Malthus?

Britain's Winston Churchill and others discovered and warned that the Anglo-American-Swiss creation, Adolf Hitler's Germany, was running out of control of its masters.

The circles of the American Museum of Natural History have contributed a leading part in imposing neo-Malthusian policies in the United States during the recent decades.

Rather than taking such wicked fellows at their words in this matter, we shall set their confessions to one side at this point in our report. Rather than examining typical, prominent personalities responsible for the present-day neo-Malthusian rampage, we shall shift our attention now to the social stratum they represent. We shall pose, and answer the question: What is the distinctive, characteristic philosophy of this social stratum, which prompts them to promote a propaganda doctrine they themselves know to be scientifically absurd?

We begin with the "case of the Reverend Professor Thomas Malthus himself. Who and what was behind his writing of his 1798 *Essay on the Principles of Population?* It was the same stratum of wealthy families behind Malthus then, which has been behind the orchestration of neo-Malthusian propaganda and movements again, today.

During the year 1751 , the leader of the cause of American Independence, Dr. Benjamin Franklin, wrote and published a pamphlet, *Observations Concerning the Increase of Mankind*, in which he argued, on premises of economic principles, for increasing rapidly the population of North America. A friend and admirer of Franklin, Gianbattista Beccaria, translated this pamphlet into Italian, and published it in Italy. The Italian edition of this pamphlet was greeted with an attempted rebuttal published by Gianmaria Ortes, a leading spokesman for the powerful rentier-financier families of Venice.

Ortes's attack on Franklin found its way to Britain, and,

at a somewhat later date, an ambitious young graduate of Oxford University's divinity school, Thomas Malthus, plagiarized and published Ortes's arguments as his own *Essay On the Principles of Population*. At that time, Malthus was in the service of the British Prime Minister, William Pitt the Younger. It was Pitt who sponsored the first, 1798 publication of Malthus's famous work. As Pitt stated to the British Parliament, it was Malthus's *On Population* which was used as pretext for the 1800 reform of the British Poor Law; Britain ceased to give financial assistance to its own "useless eaters."

That was the origin of the name "Malthusianism."

In honor of Malthus's achievement, the British East India Company created the first professorship in political economy to be established in Britain, appointing Malthus as first occupant of this position, at the Company s Haileybury College, where its own agents were trained. All the notable British economists--excepting the special case of Dr. Karl Marx--from Adam Smith and Jeremy Bentham, through John Stuart Mill, were, like Malthus, agents of the British East India Company. Most, like Bentham, Malthus, David Ricardo, James Mill and John Stuart Mill, were associated with and coordinated by Haileybury.

This connection among British political economy, Malthusianism, and the African slave-trade and China opium-trade, is indispensable for understanding the nineteenth and twentieth centuries' eruptions of Malthusianism among the English-speaking nations, for reasons we shall document here. To understand Malthusianism's influence on the continent of Europe, one must understand also the intimate connection between the backers of the Venetian Gianmaria Ortes and the British East India Company.

Who Was Behind Thomas Malthus?

British Political Economy

A relatively advanced study of political economy had been fostered in Tudor England through the influence of the Erasmians, and had continued in a vigorous form through the period of Thomas Gresham. At least, it was vigorous and competent by the standards of Europe at that time. From the time of the coronation of James VI of Scotland as King of England, in 1603, Britain dropped out of school. The teaching of modern economic science was well-advanced as a regular practice among prominent institutions of France, Italy, Germany, and Russia, more than fifty years before the first appearance of a formal doctrine of political economy in Britain.

Throughout the seventeenth and eighteenth centuries, modern political economy was taught on the continent of Europe, chiefly, under the rubric of "cameralism." This cameralism was based on such fifteenth-century pioneer economists as George Gemisthos (Plethon) and Leonardo da Vinci, as the leading work in Tudor England had been. The principles of government of the French political scientist, Jean Bodin and his *Six Books of the Commonwealth*, typified the directions of political-economic policy-making of the influential *Les Politques* of France and the republican (Commonwealth) faction in Britain. The Neapolitan school associated with Tommaso Campanella was most influential, beginning the turn of the seventeenth century. Out of the convergence of such currents emerged the political-economic policy-making of the seventeenth century *Politiques* of France, such as Richelieu, Mazarin, and the famous successor to Mazarin, Jean-Baptiste Colbert. Modern economic science proper, was developed by Gottfried Leibniz, beginning Leibniz's brief, 1671 *Society and Economy*.

The successful, early eighteenth-century development of the economy of Russia, during which the scale and quality

27

of mining and industry exceeded that in Britain, was based on Leibniz's counsel to Czar Peter I. Leibniz's economic science was taught in eighteenth-century Germany, under the title of "physical economy," as part of the cameralistic program which later produced such figures as Freiherr vom Stein and the Humboldt brothers. It was channeled in France and Italy through the Oratorian teaching-order and its orbit. It was based in Russia at Leibniz's Petrograd Academy. It was introduced into the United States before Smith's *Wealth of Nations*, chiefly through Dr. Franklin. Yet, although the house of Hanover briefly sponsored a project to make Leibniz the Prime Minister of Britain, Leibniz's economic science never reached the shores of that country.

The first effort to develop a doctrine of political economy in Britain dates from a 1763, long carriage ride, during which the notorious Second Earl of Shelburne dictated to Adam Smith the specifications for a plan to wreck the economies of the English colonies in North America. At that time, Smith was a leading subordinate of David Hume in the British Secret Intelligence Service, and formally Professor of Moral Sciences at the University of Edinburgh. Hume was Lord Shelburne's subordinate in the British Secret Intelligence Service (SIS) during operations against France, and Shelburne himself was, like his grandfather, Sir William Petty, founder of the London Royal Society, of the highest-ranking families in the Scottish branch of the SIS. Like his grandfather, Lord Shelburne was a Jesuit by reputation and background, closely linked to the same circle of French (Clermont) Jesuits as Voltaire, the French Physiocrat Quesnay, and the Jesuit-Swiss Nine Sisters' Scottish Rite Freemasonic grand lodge in Paris. He was one of that curious breed of Scottish-French-Swiss Jesuit (sometimes nominally Protestant) which, during the lifetimes of Shelburne, Franklin, and Lafayette, intersected a leading figure of that

Who Was Behind Thomas Malthus?

curious network, the Duke of Orléans.

It was David Hume who was most influential in outlining the so-called moral principles which have governed the underlying axiomatic assumptions of British political economy from Smith, through Bentham, Malthus, Ricardo, the two Mills, Jevons, Marshall, and Keynes. It is Smith's 1759 *Theory of Moral Sentiments* which supplies everything which is original in his 1776 plagiarism of A. Turgot's *Reflections on the Formation and Distribution of Wealth*, Smith's famous anti-American tract, his *Wealth of Nations*. One passage from his 1759 book is exemplary:

> . . . the care of the universal happiness of all rational and sensible beings, is the business of God and not of man. To man is alloted a much humbler department, but one much more suitable to the weakness of his powers, and to the narrowness of his comprehension: the care of his own happiness, of that of his family, his friends, his country. . . . But though we are . . . endowed with a very strong desire of those ends, it has been intrusted to the slow and uncertain determinations of our reason to find out the proper means of bringing them about. Nature has directed us to the greater part of these by original and immediate instincts. Hunger, thirst, the passion which unites the two sexes, the love of pleasure, and the dread of pain, prompt us to apply those means for their own sakes, and without any consideration of their tendency to those beneficient ends which the great Director of nature intended to produce them.

This quoted exercise in the Calvinist dogma of predestination is the essence of the rationalization which the Scottish Presbyterians and others offered in defense of such practices as the British East India Company's African slave-trade and China opium-trade. *Man, according to this Calvinist's argument, is not morally responsible for the consequences of his actions for humanity in general.* If his blind indifferentism to morality, in following nothing but his hedonistic impulses, causes cruelty and other great harm to large numbers of humanity, then God is to be blamed for having provided such a Calvinist with his hedonistic instincts.

This Calvinist's defense of immoral practices is the essence of Smith's own doctrine of the "Invisible Hand." Smith, like Hume, like Bentham, Malthus, Ricardo, James Mill's defense of genocide against peoples of India in 1819, John Stuart Mill's doctrine of "utility," and the work of Jevons, Marshall, and Keynes, among others, bases himself on that radical rejection of any knowable moral law by David Hume, that moral "indifferentism" which enraged Immanuel Kant to write his own *Critique of Pure Reason* against British empiricism.

More significant than Smith in the history of British political economy, is the most intimate of Lord Shelburne's accomplices and protégés, Jeremy Bentham. Bentham's theme is the same cited from Smith's 1759 text, but Bentham is more savagely to the point, more radical a follower of Hume. On this account, Smith's 1759 text is to be compared immediately with Bentham's 1780 *Introduction to the Principles of Morals and Legislation*, and Bentham's principal text explicitly on the subject of political economy, his 1787 *In Defense of Usury*. Otherwise typical of Bentham's radicalism is his *In Defense of Pederasty*, and his design for a brainwashing prison suited for the society of George Orwell's 1984, the *Panopticon*.

This was the prevailing moral philosophy among those

Who Was Behind Thomas Malthus?

circles which adopted the Venetian Gianmaria Ortes's policy as British Malthusianism. Before turning to the immediate circumstances under which Malthus's book appeared, we show the character of the connection to Venice.

During the interval 1589 to 1603, the Venetian and Genoese financial "black nobility" of Italy and adjoining countries conducted a bloody struggle within England, to discredit and destroy Elizabeth I's designated heir to her throne, the boy Essex, and to secure the succession for the Genoese asset, James VI of Scotland. Genoa had controlled Scotland since its mercenary forces, Robert Bruce and his Templars, had subjugated the nation during the early fourteenth century, and controlled Scotland's principal connections on the continent, the French-speaking areas of Switzerland and adjoining portions of France, since the period of the fifteenth century when Britain, Genoa, and Charles the Bold of Burgundy had been allied against France's Louis XI.

Following his coronation in 1603, King James I of England granted his foreign financial backers a tax-farming monopoly over the public debt and tax collections of England. The Francis Bacon who had been a leading asset of the Genoese (Pallavicini) interest in the 1589-1603 coup d'état, was made the Chancellor of the Exchequer, until public opinion refused to tolerate any longer Bacon's rampaging embezzlements. Out of this came the seventeenth-century Civil War in Britain, and the foundations of the City of London's financial center and the Bank of England.

As part of the same process, the Genoese and Venetian financial interests moved the Atlantic division of their Levant Company, from its ruinously looted base in Portugal, to Britain and the Netherlands, where this Levant Company produced the British and Dutch East India

31

Company, an arrangement consolidated with the reforms of 1688-1689. This is what Hume and Shelburne represented; it was the British East India Company which consolidated its grip over the British government by Shelburne's agreement with King George III of 1782-1783.

A few observations on the period 1603-1783 must be added, so that the character of the British and U.S.A. backers of neo-Malthusianism today may be accurately understood.

As we have noted, the takeover of Britain by foreign, Genoese and Venetian interests, was directly as well as indirectly the cause of the seventeenth-century Civil War in England. It was the fall of the Commonwealth, with the Stuart Restoration of 1660, which accelerated the emigration of British republicans into the colonies in North America. These 1603-1689 developments determined the profound difference in culture generally, and moral philosophy which increasingly separated Britain from America during the eighteenth century.

In Britain, over the course of the late seventeenth and eighteenth centuries, the foreign-controlled ruling interests became so dominant and so integrated into the ruling landed and financial aristocracies, that what had been once foreign and what domestic became more or less indistinguishable, at least to the degree the Scottish and English components of the British ruling strata were united in policy. The persistence of this rule, and the top-down impact on popular life, transformed the British subjects in philosophical outlook, to the point that nineteenth-century British subjects, like those of today, accept the immoral dogma of Hume, Smith, Bentham, et al. As "common sense" and "human nature." Except for a vestige of republicanism in England, typified by Franklin's friend, Dr. Joseph Priestley, and Irish and Scottish republicanism, by the 1790s the philosophical outlook of John Milton was

Who Was Behind Thomas Malthus?

nearly eradicated among the population of Britain.

The republican circles of North America became thus the center of republican philosophy and culture among the English-speaking peoples. The effects of this philosophical difference upon the respective practices of the two nations are typified by evidence from the U.S. census of 1790 and correlated evidence of that period. The U.S. adult population had a literacy rate in excess of 90 percent, more than twice that in Britain. Exemplary of this, the American was known widely throughout Europe as "the Latin farmer" because of the degree of familiarity with classics among U.S. citizens. The leading political literature, the popular literature which won support for the U.S. Constitution, for example, shows that the adult Americans of the 1790s were vastly superior to those of today, in terms of that quality which Percy B. Shelley defines as the "power to receive and impart profound conceptions respecting man and nature." This cultural superiority of the American citizen over the British subject during that period was echoed in the fact that the Americans produced and received as income twice the amounts of wealth of the British. Insofar as the American patriots were of English origin--and many of them were of Scottish and German origins--they were the followers of John Milton, to the point, that in that sense, the American Revolution was a successful repetition of the seventeenth--century Civil War in Britain.

These developments in Britain and America were situated within the general pattern of developments in Europe as a whole during these two centuries. It is in this context, that the connection of the Venetian, Genoese-Swiss, and British financial oligarchies is most clearly shown.

The same circumstances underlying the Genoese coup d'état of 1589-1603 in England prompted the seventeenth-century Catholic monarchs of France to lead the Protestant

League of Europe, a leadership shaped successively by Cardinal Richelieu, by the Pope's own appointed successor to Richelieu, Cardinal Mazarin, and Mazarin's successor, Jean-Baptiste Colbert. The Catholic Party of Europe, led by the Venetians' assets, the Habsburgs, included the French-speaking Swiss Protestants as well as the Venetian Jesuits, and also, usually, the Protestant monarchies of Britain and the Netherlands--when French bribes in the pocket did not outweigh avowed loyalties in the consciences of the Restoration Stuarts. If the labels from that period are therefore often outrageously misleading, such is the commonplace state of leading political affairs in history, into the present day.

The real issues of the sixteenth and seventeenth centuries' wars in Europe were not between Catholics as Catholics and Protestants as Protestants. The ranks of both Protestants and Catholics were bitterly divided against themselves on issues more fundamental than the matter of nominal adherence to the Papacy. The one view, among both Catholics and Protestants, is efficiently traced back through the 1439 Council of Florence. It is the viewpoint of fifteenth-century Catholic, neo-Platonic humanism, as epitomized by the powerfully influential writings of Cardinal Nicholas of Cusa on theology, natural law, and scientific method. The opposing view, erupting afresh as Venetian and Genoese policy, was a revival of the standpoint of Roman imperial law, the View of man, and of man in the universe traditionally associated with Byzantine, Roman, Persian, Babylonian empires, and the ancient Philistine city of Tyre, a tradition traced to the Chaldeans of Ur.

The first, republican view, is founded on the premise that the human individual is absolutely distinguished from the beasts by virtue of a divine potentiality, on whose account human life is sacred to society, and for which

Who Was Behind Thomas Malthus?

reason the function of the state is to protect and develop those creative-mental potentialities of each and every member of society, and to afford those developed potentialities protected opportunity for fruitful expression. The opposing, oligarchical view of man, like that of Bacon, Hobbes, Locke, Hume, and Bentham, views man as a hedonistic variety of talking beast, whose knowledge and self-interest are limited to perceptions of pleasure and pain. That oligarchical, degraded view of man is expressed by the cited passage from Adam Smith. It is expressed succinctly also by Bentham's *Introduction to Principles of Morals and Legislation.*

During the same period as Malthus produced his *On Population*, the essential political division within European civilization was described by the poet, dramatist, and historian, Friedrich Schiller, as a division between the republican tradition of Solon of Athens, and the oligarchical tradition of the mythical Lycurgus of Sparta. The republican tradition, in the proper, broad usage of this term for that philosophical outlook, is traced in Western Europe through the influence of St. Augustine's writings, the great reforms of Charlemagne, and Cusa's elaboration of the principles of natural law upon which constitutions of nations and the law among nations are defined in principle. On the opposing, oligarchical side, it is the rampant sodomy of the Spartan aristocracy, whose young aristocrats killed enslaved helots at whim, to keep the helot population in check, which aptly expresses the policies and practices of the Venetians' Habsburg-led "Catholic Party" of the sixteenth and seventeenth centuries.

It is from the philosophical outlook typified by Lycurgus's Sparta, and evil creator of the "Spartan model," the temple of the Cult of Apollo, at Delphi, that modern Malthusianism and neo-Malthusianism are produced. This is most directly illustrated by consulting the writings of the

There Are No Limits to Growth

leading apologist for the philosophical outlook of Delphi, Aristotle, especially his evil *Politics* and *Nicomachean Ethics*. There is no evil practiced by the Malthusians' factional forces which is not recommended in those latter two literary sources. This is the standpoint of David Hume, of Adam Smith, of Jeremy Bentham, and Lord Shelburne's circle generally. This is the moral-philosophical standpoint of the British East India Company then, and the neo-Malthusians now.

Before turning to the U.S. backers of Malthusianism, one additional set of facts concerning Malthus's immediate orbit is indispensable: How the British East India Company took control of the British government over the interval 1782-1783.

By 1782, the war against the United States had brought the indebted British government to the point of bankruptcy. In this period, Shelburne made several attempts to gain control over the government. His efforts of 1783-1784 succeeded. Together with Francis Baring, banker of the British East India Company, Shelburne negotiated an agreement with King George III which placed Shelburne's tool, William Pitt the Younger, in the position of First Treasury Lord. This was only the first step. According to surviving records, the grand total of the sum which John Robinson paid on Shelburne's behalf, to buy up the entire British Parliament of 1784 was £200,000; Laurence Sullavan of the British East India Company arranged the financing of this purchase. So, Shelburne's tool, William Pitt the Younger, began his long rule as Prime Minister.

During the same year, 1784, Shelburne launched his reorganization of the British East India Company itself, giving it increased powers and wealth, and consolidating its position as virtually identical with the British Secret Intelligence Service. Jeremy Bentham emerged as Shelburne's leading specialist in dirty tricks--including, in

Who Was Behind Thomas Malthus?

due course, sending the British SIS agents, Danton and the Swiss Marat, from their training stations in London, to lead the Jacobin Terror in France. This was the establishment of which Malthus, Ricardo, James Mill, John Stuart Mill, and others were assimilated as officials. *These were the Malthusians*.

These men were Jesuits. Contrary to the official history of the Jesuits, the order was actually created, not in Paris, but by the Contarini family of Venice in Venice itself. Ignatius Loyola, on a pilgrimage to Palestine, was held over in Venice, and recruited to head up a Venice-created secret intelligence service modeled in all essential features on the intelligence service of the ancient Cult of Delphi, the Peripatetics. The Jesuit order was originally a spin-off from the Hospitaller Order of St. John, at the time known as the Order of Malta, which was itself controlled by Venice. For good reasons, the Papacy suppressed the Jesuits during the eighteenth century, and the order's headquarters was moved to Russia, where it remained (at least, officially) until the Venetian Capodistria's direction over the 1815 Congress of Vienna facilitated bringing the Jesuits back to power in Western Europe, where the order functioned as the secret intelligence arm of Prince Metternich, and became engaged, in this capacity, as an accomplice of the British SIS in the wave of assassinations and assassination attempts against President Abraham Lincoln and members of his government.

Sir William Petty, Lord Shelburne's grandfather, was trained under Mersenne's direction at the Jesuit college at Caen, where the Jesuit agent René Descartes had been trained. The inner circle of the Scottish crew which Charles II brought back to Britain in 1660 were Jesuit agents. Shelburne himself was Jesuit-trained in France, and was kept from topmost official positions in Britain chiefly because of the popular sentiments on the subject of Jesuits.

There Are No Limits to Growth

More concretely, Shelburne was a product of the Bolingbroke circle, to which he was linked in France through his father-in-law, John Cataret. Later, Benjamin Disraeli summed up the matter:

> Lord Shelburne adopted from the first the Bolingbroke system; a real royalty, in lieu of the chief magistratry; a permanent alliance with France instead of the Whig scheme of viewing in that power that natural enemy of England; and, above all, a plan of commercial freedom, the germ of which may be found in the long-maligned negotiations of Utrecht, but which, in the instance of Lord Shelburne, were soon in time matured by all the economical science of Europe.

Disraeli gilds, not the lily, but the toad. Shelburne's alliance with France was with the Duke of Orléans, anti-Franklin France, and with the Grand Priory of the Order of St. John in France. These were the forces which overthrew and beheaded King Louis XVI and Marie Antoinette, which directed the rise of the Jacobins to power, and the Jacobin Terror, and which brought to power, beginning 1786, the "free trade" policy and Finance Minister, Jacques Necker, by means of which the most powerful industrial nation of Europe, France, was bankrupted in 1789. This was all accomplished in concert with the (then officially suppressed) Jesuits, and the leading Swiss banking families based in Geneva and Lausanne.

The same Hospitaller order from which the Jesuits were taken as a peripatetic rib, today fly their flag over Switzerland, and gave that nation the education of the John Calvin who was trained in the same Paris operations which sent Ignatius Loyola to Venice. So, Genoese Geneva became nominally Protestant, and Genoese-owned Scotland

Who Was Behind Thomas Malthus?

became Presbyterian, whereas anti-Papacy Venice deployed a nominally Catholic Jesuit order. In France, where the Scottish Rite, the Jesuits, and the Swiss Calvinists were invariably allies in the same wicked operations, under the umbrella of the Grand Priory of St. John, there were no functional differences among the three. These gentlemen were governed by common principles which they viewed in practice as a higher degree of faith than their respective nominal professions to a Protestant or Catholic denomination. The same is true in France today, and also in the United States, at least at the highest ranks of the Scottish Rite and Hospitallers. This is part of the key to Malthusianism, including *the Jesuit order's shameless promotion of the Club of Rome within the precincts of official institutions of the Vatican itself*, reaching even into the Pontifical Academy of Science--little wonder the Church's attempts to combat Malthusian anti-life dogmas have so often seemed to fail for mysterious causes.

As to whether some members of the Jesuit order, or ordinary Presbyterians or Scottish Rite Freemasons are respectively Christian or Judaic in any strict sense of the terms, we are not attempting to determine here. We are not meddling into the internal affairs of organized religions, but merely noting meddling in the name of religious bodies into policies of nations, and, in this instance, in a very wicked fashion. The fact is, as we have indicated, that the Jesuit order as an order, the upper ranks of the Scottish Rite as a Jesuit-created Rosicrucian cult, and the banking circles united as the Calvinists of the Church of Scotland or of French-speaking Switzerland and France, are consistently one and the same force dedicated to Malthusianism and related projects. Shelburne's case is the evil epitome of the worst in each of them all.

These fine gentlemen established their greater power over Britain, and within the United States, beginning 1787-

1792, beginning with British Secretary Henry Dundas's master plan for expanding the opium-trade into China. So, the British East India Company, following in the footsteps of the Dutch East India Company before it, shifted its investments from the perishable cargo of the African slave-trade into the more compact, and vastly more lucrative China opium-trade. It had been the Jesuits, during their operations in China and India during the seventeenth and eighteenth centuries, who had made the organization of this traffic possible on such a scale.

Such is the character of these Malthusians. Adam Smith had defended the opium-trade in a manner consistent with his Scottish Calvinist's Jesuitical morality:

> "the care of the universal happiness of all rational and sensible beings, is the business of God and not of man. To man is allotted a much humbler department . . . to apply these means [immoral hedonism] for their own sakes, and *without any consideration of their tendency to those beneficent ends which the great Director of nature intended to produce by* [such hedonistic instincts]."

In the case of the British East India company and its American agents, the African slave-trade and China opium-trade, and, in the case of the leading American families, treason, were pursuits of profit by means of which they and their descendants might become wealthier, more powerful, and even all the more paragons of respectability.

The African slave-trade, the China opium-trade, monstrous usury, and the profitable occupation of treason, were the hallmarks of moral character and philosophy of the British East India Company and its American agents. These were the Malthusians then; their descendants, and the Swiss and "black nobility" descendants, are the force

Who Was Behind Thomas Malthus?

behind neo-Malthusianism today.

The Opium-Trafficking Families of New England

The kernel of what is called the "Eastern Establishment" in the United States today is pivoted around a collection of "great American family fortunes" amassed chiefly from those families' leading participation in the U.S. side of the British East India Company's China opium-trade of the late eighteenth and the nineteenth centuries, chiefly the "Perkins Syndicate" based in Salem, Massachusetts. These are the Lowells, the Cabots, the Forbeses, the Higginsons, the Peabodys, the Cushings, and the Perkinses, a collection of families originally, chiefly, from Essex County, north of Boston, in Massachusetts, and so incestuously intermarried since the time of the 1776-1783 U.S. war with Britain, they all, including the nominal "Lowell," McGeorge Bundy, are part of one and the same biological family today.

From the first appearance of these New England families as a distinctive force, during the 1763-1783 period, they enjoyed in common the distinctions of having opposed American Independence, of profiting as agents of British influence during the period 1776-1815 even to the point of outright treason, and of having accumulated their principal fortunes from: real estate speculations aided by the British government, legalized piracy (privateering), the African slave-trade, and the China opium-trade.

The collection is also distinguished by several additional notable features. They were linked to the British agent Aaron Burr during the period of the American Revolution, and were also backers of Burr in treasonous plots specifically dated to 1800, 1804, and 1807-1808. This Essex Junto, as John Quincy Adams and the U.S. secret intelligence service uncovered the name for their

plotting, were constantly operating in collusion with not

41

only Burr's circles, but also British secret intelligence operatives based in Nova Scotia and Boston. During the second official U.S. war with Britain, in 1812-1815, these families were supplying funds and matériel to the British forces based in Canada then invading the United States. During the same period, they were associated with a project called the "Hartford Convention," a new plot to split New England from the United States and form a Confederacy together with British provinces in Canada.

The consistent object of their treasonous plotting, in cooperation with British SIS, during the entire span from 1800 through 1862, was to split the United States into two or more, "balkanized" sections. This was the object of their backing of Aaron Burr's candidacy for President in 1800; of Burr's campaign to become Governor of New York State, and split the United States from that post, in 1804; in the new effort to split the Union in 1807-1808--stopped by cooperation between President Thomas Jefferson and then-Senator John Quincy Adams; and, in their creation of the Confederate States of America, in cooperation with SIS, as the final effort in this direction.

On the latter, briefly. The Essex Junto, operating chiefly out of Salem and Newburyport, created a nest in Charleston, South Carolina, in cooperation with British SIS. This nest was used to organize a network of Scottish Rite Freemasons throughout the southern states, together with satellite Freemasonic organizations such as the Knights of the Golden Circle, the predecessor organization for British SIS's creation of the Ku Klux Klan in 1867. The Newburyport center of this operation, featuring the families' spokesman, Caleb Cushing, steered the pathway into the 1861-1865 Civil War in concert with his co-plotters in Charleston, South Carolina, and with the chief British agent in New York City, August Belmont. (All the reports given here are documented by correspondence of the principals, including Belmont's, surviving today from the

Who Was Behind Thomas Malthus?

indicated period.) Belmont was kingmaker of the Democratic Party during the 1850s and 1860s. These plotters put two successive Presidents into office, their agents Franklin Pierce and James Buchanan, and used these two administrations to arm the future Confederacy and disarm the future Union forces. To heat up the situation, the New Englanders from the African slave-trade (and China opium-trade) became "radical Abolitionists," steered from Britain, organizing various anti-slavery paramilitary operations, including their agent John Brown's, to foment the circumstances under whose passions North and South could be matured to a point of willingness for separation.

Throughout this, the Essex Junto, with its allies in New Hampshire, Vermont, and Connecticut, were in close cooperation with British-linked financial interests in New York City, New Jersey, and Pennsylvania.

The foundations of their great fortunes, from the China opium-trade, were established beginning 1792, when Thomas Handasyd Perkins, of Salem, Massachusetts, shifted out of the African slave-trade, where his James and T. H. Perkins and Company had built up their initial fortune, into the British East India Company's China opium-trade. Perkins's initial financial success in this new venture had the advantage of being conducted with cooperation of members of the Perkins family who had fled to Britain during the American Revolution. All of the New England "families" were either directly or indirectly intermarried—massively--into British families. The British side of the family ran the opium-traffic out of the Turkish port of Smyrna, the original source of supply for Perkins's operations.

All the New England "families" of the Essex Junto and its added adjuncts participated with Perkins, thus forming the "Perkins Syndicate." Perkins soon out-distanced the New York opium trader, Jacob Astor. Russel and Company, the leading Connecticut opium-trader, was adjunct to the Perkins operations.

It was, as we have reported, one incestuously intermarried mass constituting a common extended family. McGeorge Bundy is nominally a "Lowell," a family traced from the Bristol African slave-trading port in England, to Newburyport. Bundy is therefore among the heirs to the estate produced by treasonous real estate speculations, outright treason, the African slave-trade, the China opium-trade, the child labor of the Lowells' New England textile mills, of the New England fishing industry, and so forth. Yet, the name "Lowell" really is no distinction at all. Shake Bundy's family tree, and all the rotten apples of treason-ridden New England "families" fall out.

In addition to the New England "families," and the New York and other families associated with the original Aaron Burr network, there are two principal categories of additions added to establish the core of the "Eastern Establishment" today. In some cases, such as the house of Morgan, the new "families" were created as joint operations of the British and New England, or the New York, New Jersey, and Pennsylvania, or the special gang around Baltimore, Maryland. In a second categorical case, the networks of agents deployed by August Belmont, Judah Benjamin, and the Slidells in building the Confederacy, enriched themselves by looting their former neighbors in the post-Civil War "carpetbagging" operations, to form the kernel of the New York investment banking community today. Into this general mass were added "families" from, chiefly, Switzerland, Germany, and Britain.

This mass was whipped into its present shape by successive operations run chiefly from Britain during the past hundred years. Two instances are most notable. The first was the establishment of the National Civic Federation, chiefly by the Morgan interests, as a colonial

Who Was Behind Thomas Malthus?

branch of Lord Alfred Milner's London Round Table organization. After World War I, Milner sponsored a second association in Britain, based at the old Pitt residence in London, Chatham House, the Royal Institute for International Affairs, whose New York City branch became the New York Council on Foreign Relations, absorbing the National Civic Federation into it.

These "families" are generally organized on the basis of the "Venetian model," the *fondo*. A *fondo* is a financial trust, from which the heirs may enjoy the use of assigned properties and may draw income, but may not, individually draw down the capital. Through the *fondo*, the "family" enjoys what may appear an approximation of an "immortal existence," an existence which is more or less independent of the fate of the existing generation of the biological family associated with the *fondo*. The *fondo* is managed "professionally" by a group of persons which may or may not include members of the biological family, and in the Italian model, the executive of the *fondo* has the powers of a Roman *paterfamilias*, including the power to adopt an heir from outside the ranks of the biological family, to the purpose of perpetuating the *fondo*'s legal existence.

On this account, the "family" has the appearance of a feudal institution, on which grounds the leading American economist, Henry C. Carey, defined the British economy as not capitalist, but of a mixed, feudal-capitalist variety, in which the feudal interest--the rentier-financier interest of ruling financial "families"--held the subordinated, industrial-capitalist interest its virtual slave.

It is an institutional form much older than Venice, or even its appearance as the ruling strata of oligarchical power in the Roman Empire. It is as old as the ancient Phoenicians, and the Chaldeans of Ur, at a minimum. *It is the characteristic social institution of an oligarchical form of society.*

There Are No Limits to Growth

From the most ancient times for which records exist, the oligarchical "family" has had the same essential characteristics familiar from the case of Venice. These families despise investment in capital of production, except as such investments may be subordinate and useful to a form of financial investment which they prefer. Their preferred investments, over the millennia to date, have been *usury, appreciation of ground-rent-income, monopolistic profits of commodity price-speculation*, especially in raw materials-traffic, the luxury goods trade, and, the power and wealth obtained directly and indirectly through *tax-farming of the public debt and public revenues of governments*. It was the Phoenicians who pioneered in developing the African slave-trade, and Arab traders whose practices were shaped by the Phoenician tradition who originated the drug-traffic into the Far East, as well as building up the African slave-trade to the levels from which the Venetians expanded it.

In U.S. legal practice, especially since the introduction of the personal income tax, attorneys---including a significant number from the ranks of the families and their special law firms, have devised various ruses for enabling the families to establish forms equivalent to the *fondo*: remainder-trusts in real estate, and private family foundations, are merely illustrative cases. Hence the "families" *represented* in the circles of the New York Council on Foreign Relations are represented more or less in a Venetian way; it is the *fondi*, or at least their American legal approximation, which are represented. It is the *fondi* of the "Eastern Establishment," together with their adjuncts, which believe themselves to exert concerted, syndicated rule over the United States, to rig its elections, and to otherwise determine the rise and fall of its legal governments.

It would be an error to assume that the characteristic

Who Was Behind Thomas Malthus?

features of the "Eastern Establishment" families are determined merely by the combinations of biological descent and the financial forms in which the "family" is perpetuated with or despite the heirs. Church and school are the keys. Today, the "families" are chiefly Anglican (Church of England), Presbyterian (Church of Scotland), or Catholic (Jesuit, Venetian). The overall structure is glued together by "fraternal" cults intersecting the priestly and lay hierarchies of the churches. At the top rank of the cults is the British Order of St. John (Hospitallers), underneath which are located, and intersecting with it, the Scottish Rite Freemasonry's top ranks, and the Jesuit order. This religious and cult side of the operation intersects key universities, such as Harvard, Yale, Princeton, the so-called "Ivy League" colleges, and, to some degree, a network of private secondary schools, such as the famous Anglican Groton, and the Phillips Academy at Andover and Exeter. The family circle, the church, the fraternal associations, the universities, and the university's alumni club, provide the new individuals of the "Eastern Establishment" families a more or less controlled social environment from birth to death.

This configuration of institutional influences is chiefly modeled upon the British example, most emphatically so since Elliot became President of Harvard University. It functions as a transmission belt for imposing cultural matrices upon the mind of the member of the family, to the effect that the member so conditioned "thinks like a member of the Establishment," shares the cultural and philosophical outlook assigned to his or her generation of the families.

This same controlled social environment serves an additional function: screening and recruiting prospective servants of the families. The universities, the churches, and the fraternal associations (cults) serve as the principal vehicles for this process. A prospective talent may be "looked over" at convenience, without implying any commitment to offering a position in service of the family. Prospective recruits may be "groomed," and possible appointments may be "introduced," and so forth and so on. Key academic figures in universities, and "spotters" in other educational institutions, serve as screening agents and recruiters of individuals to be added to what is in effect a feudal bureaucracy of persons whose careers are dependent upon service to the "families."

This process of acculturation over more than two hundred years, since Lord Shelburne's operations first acquired the kernel of the future "American families," has thus transmitted to the present generation of the "Eastern Establishment" the same general philosophical world outlook earlier expressed by slave-trading, opium-trading, and treason. The point is not that the ancestors of many among the leading figures of the Eastern Establishment were slave-traders, opium- traders, and traitors; the point is that the process of acculturation we have indicated briefly here has transmitted the same morality, the same philosophical outlook to the enlarged ranks of the "families" and their "feudal-bureaucratic" appendages today.

This "Eastern Establishment" controls most of news and entertainment media of the United States, most of the leading financial institutions, most of the corporations controlling raw materials, has a top-down grip on the real estate market, especially real estate holdings in mineral and other special kinds of natural resources, and a grip on most industrial corporations otherwise, either directly or through financing. These forces generally control most leading circles of the political parties, control the politically and culturally influential foundations, and so forth and so on.

These are the forces of the Eastern Establishment within

the United States who pushed through a sharp change in U.S. policy during 1964-1968, shifting the U.S. toward becoming a neo-Malthusians' paradise, the wreckage of a "post-industrial society." McGeorge Bundy, the "head of the establishment," was foremost in those operations, first as National Security Council head under Presidents Kennedy and Johnson, later during his long reign, beginning 1966, at the Ford Foundation, and more recently, on a Sloan family funding, as a senior schemer elevated to the higher rank of "wise old man," in a special nest created for him at New York University. Bundy and his crew organized the instant-creation of the "environmentalist movement" out of the rubbles of the Ban the Bomb, anti-Vietnam War, and New Left generally, over the winter of 1969-1970.

There was a deeper aspect to this process, to which we will turn our attention now, in the following chapter, where we shall examine the long-range strategy of which the present neo-Malthusian onslaughts are merely an essential aspect.

Bertrand Russell, the relatively pacifist philosopher who demanded a preventive nuclear war during 1946-49, before going on to organize the "Ban the Bomb" movement and the Pugwash Conferences.

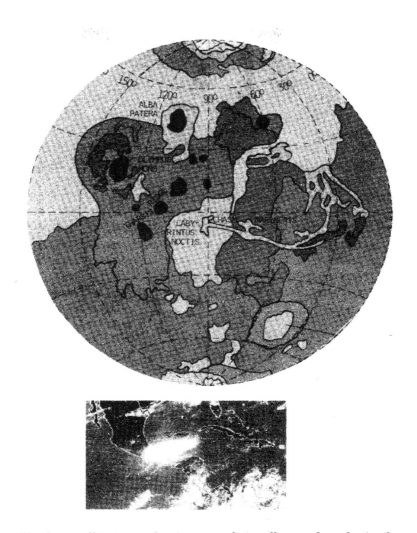

Weather satellite image showing natural air pollutants from the April 4, 1982 eruption of the El Chichón volcano in Mexico. The bright circular dot at Mexico's isthmus shown in the top rectangle, a cloud of fine ash and sulfur dioxide, had expanded, within twelve hours, to the wide region shown in the bottom rectangle. An estimated 15 million tons of sulfur and its compounds was spread around the globe in this massive act of pollution by "Mother Nature."

Building on the re-establishment of scientific rigor by Cardinal Nicholas of Cusa (bottom right), modern economic science in the strict sense was developed by Gottfried Wilhelm Leibniz (top right). Benjamin Franklin seized on Leibniz's ideas and realized them in the American Revolution.

Jesuit founder Ignatius Loyola (above left) and Protestant John Calvin (right)—two sides of the same evil coin. Below, Lord Shelburne (left) and his "secret weapon" against the American Revolution, Adam Smith.

The oligarchs are the enemies of human development. Above, the family of Charles IV, Hapsburg emperor of Spain, as painted by Francisco Goya. Below, W. Averell Harriman.

Venice (above) seat of the old family funds, the *fondi*. Below, the Holy Mountain, Mount Athos, their organizing center for the spread of evil pagan cults of the Gnostic variety.

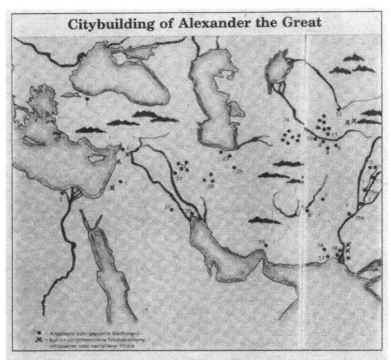

The city-building program of Alexander the Great. Dots show the site of Alexander's planned cities.

On March 23, 1983, President Ronald Reagan declared that the military strategy of "Mutally Assured Destruction"—MAD—ought to be replaced with a strategy of "Mutually Assured Survival," based on the development of directed energy beam anti-missile weapons like the artist's conception shown here. Will the policy adopted from LaRouche's 1982 proposal be carried through?

For Thomas Malthus (1766-1820), the East India Company created his own chair of Political Economy at the firm's own school, Haileybury College. With his tract, *Essay on the Principles of Population,* Malthus propagandized to justify the policies of the East India Company: the Slave Trade and the Opium Trade.

3

Bertrand Russell's Dream of World-Empire

Most people unfamiliar with the truth about the late Bertrand Russell sincerely believe that the grandson of British Prime Minister Lord John Russell was a peace-loving fellow. They either do not remember, or simply overlook the fact that it was Bertrand Russell who attempted to mobilize Britain, the United States, France, and so forth, for a "preventive nuclear war" back during the 1946-1949 period. Not only did Russell campaign for such a war; he was nearly successful. The United States and Britain did commit themselves to a war plan for such a war; the war plan was named "Operation Dropshot," and outlined preparations for a nuclear war to be launched by the second half of the 1950s.

What stopped the "preventive nuclear war" against the Soviet Union was not a twinge of conscience on Russell's part. When the Soviet Union developed a fission weapon about 1949, "ten years before expected," and next developed deployable H-bomb weapons, about the same time that the group led by Dr. Edward Teller succeeded in the United States, the idea of fighting a "preventive war"-- in which only one side had nuclear weapons--was no longer possible. Russell went back to parading himself as a pacifist again, and organized his international Ban the Bomb movement of the 1950s.

Nonetheless, the long-range policy which prompted Russell to demand "preventive nuclear war" continued, and became the strategic doctrine known by such various names

There Are No Limits to Growth

as Nuclear Deterrence, Mutual and Assured Destruction (MAD), Limited Nuclear War, Forward Nuclear Defense, Flexible Response, and Détente. It was this strategic doctrine which was the premise for shifting the world into a neo-Malthusian policy during the 1964-1968 period.

It began in October 1946, in the form of an article by Bertrand Russell published in the *Bulletin of the Atomic Scientists*. The roots of Russell's thinking during this period go deep into his own personal past, deeper into the aspects of the history of Britain we briefly identified in the preceding chapter, and on principle go deep into periods of history when the inhabitants of Britain were celebrating, it is told, human sacrifices at Stonehenge. For the moment, we shall take the history prior to 1964 for granted, and limit our attention for a while to the immediate facts of the post-war period.

Russell's general proposal throughout this period was that the development of nuclear weapons had created the situation in which it had become necessary to establish a world-government which would have a monopoly on possession and use of such weapons. His proposal for a "preventive nuclear war" against the Soviet Union was a by-product of his proposal for world-government. To create a world-government with a nuclear weapons monopoly, he argued, it was indispensable to conquer the Soviet Union before it developed such weapons: After the build-up of a nuclear arsenal by the Western Alliance had reached the point of readiness for a decisive assault, overwhelming Soviet land-based and other "conventional" military forces, the war should be launched. Once the preventive nuclear war were won, the proposed form of world-government could be established by the victorious allied forces.

To foster this general policy, Russell organized an association called the World Association of

Bertrand Russell's Dream of World Empire

Parliamentarians for World Government (WAPWG). Russell's WAPWG lingered on into its 1955 conference, in which four Soviet representatives participated, two of whom would appear later as participants in another series of conferences, the latter to become known as the Pugwash Conferences. Russell's aim of establishing world-government was not dropped at that point; it reemerged in the modified form typified by the Pugwash Conferences. After 1955, the WAPWG itself retreated from prominence; the Pugwash Conferences took over.

The crucial early developments within the context of the Pugwash Conferences occurred at the second Pugwash Conference, held in Quebec, Canada, in 1958. The most important of the items of the agenda of this 1958 session was a speech on the subject of "How to Live With The Bomb--and Survive," delivered by Dr. Leo Szilard, a veteran atomic scientist from the University of Chicago. An Austro-Hungarian by origin--a fact of some significance in itself--Szilard had passed part of his emigré life in Britain, also significant, before moving on to the United States. This 1958 address by Szilard, later published in a 1966 issue of the *Bulletin of the Atomic Scientists*, became the inspiration for the famous motion-picture, "Dr. Strangelove," in which the late British actor, Peter Sellers, performed several parts, including his famous caricature of Leo Szilard as "Strangelove."

The leading features of the proposed policy which Szilard outlined in that address included these. (1) To ensure world peace by using nuclear weapons as a mutual deterrence against the launching of general war by either superpower. (2) The occurrence of limited nuclear wars as a device for easing tensions, and thus avoiding the accumulation of tensions to the level at which general nuclear war occurred. (3) The willingness of the United States, for example, to permit Soviet thermonuclear destruction of one selected city, if necessary, to balance off Soviet injuries suffered in localized warfare. (4) Generalized Middle East petroleum crises, leading into a general destruction of the Middle East.

It should not be necessary to do more than mention the fact, that what Szilard outlined became the adopted policies of the U.S.A. and the NATO alliance over the course of the 1960s. The same was true of other Pugwash Conferences. It has been generally the case, that policies adopted by the Pugwash Conferences' sessions, over the 1960s, and 1970s, have become the strategic and foreign policy doctrine of the U.S.A. and the NATO alliance.

We describe the Pugwash Conferences more exactly. It was a regular meeting of representatives of the Soviet Union, Britain, and the U.S. Eastern Establishment, at which the body negotiated agreements to strategic military and foreign policies, policies later successfully imposed upon the governments of the United States and the NATO countries by agents such as Robert S. McNamara, McGeorge Bundy, and Henry A. Kissinger.

This general sort of Anglo-American negotiation with Soviet representatives is usually called a "back-channel" negotiation. "Back-channel" negotiations and other exchanges of views are neither good nor bad in and of themselves. Private exchanges of that sort could be, and sometimes are, useful ways of conducting the kinds of exploratory discussions which could not occur under official, diplomatic auspices.

However, the Pugwash Conferences were not any ordinary sort of "back-channel" discussion process. It was a place at which private interests of the Anglo-American establishments met to plot the future of the world with the Soviet government, *behind the back of the government of the United States.* In effect, the Soviet government was

Bertrand Russell's Dream of World Empire

participating in dictating the military and foreign policies of the United States, without knowledge of this fact by those U.S. governments to which such cooked-up policies were "sold" as clever ways of frustrating Soviet interests and ambitions.

There were certain other features to these Pugwash negotiations which explain the peculiar character of these negotiations. There were certain features of these negotiations which no U.S. President was supposed to recognize--until it was too late. The long-term objective of these Pugwash Conferences was the establishment of a system of world-government. Leo Szilard had already recommended this back in his 1958 address; he had proposed that Nuclear Deterrence must lead into a redrawing of the political map of the world, an enterprise which Britain's Lord Peter Carrington has named a "New Yalta" policy.

That, however, merely scratches the surface of the matter. What was being negotiated was the establishment of a system of world-government, in which the world as a whole would be divided among two, or possibly three world-empires, depending upon-whether or not China was awarded its own sphere of influence over such neighboring areas as Japan, Southeast Asia, and perhaps parts of India. Excepting the special case of China, the rest of the world was to be divided between a Western and Eastern division of world-empire, two systems of world-government, one ruled by the wealthy rentier families of the West, the other by the Russian Empire to the East.

This proposal has a more or less exact precedent in European history. Surviving copies of the correspondence exist, documenting the plan to divide the Persian Empire of the mid-fourth century B.C. into two parts. The two parts were to be divided by a line defined by the Euphrates River, with a corresponding division of Anatolia into a western and eastern portion. The existing Persian Empire of the Achaemenids was to retain the area to the east of the Euphrates River, and a corresponding, eastern portion of Anatolia. A Western Division of the Persian Empire, to be given to the hereditary rulership of King Philip of Macedon, was to be developed west of that dividing line. As part of the agreement, Philip was to impose upon the Western Division a political, social and economic system which the correspondence describes sometimes as the "Persian Model," and in other locations, the "Oligarchical Model"; the two terms have the same meaning. What these terms meant, is described in considerable detail by one of the leading agents involved in this plot, by Aristotle, in his *Politics* and *Nicomachean Ethics*.

This plan was devised by the real rulers of the Persian Empire, the combination of rentier-financier families and pagan priesthood known to the present day as the "Chaldeans," and also known by such names as "Magicians," "Phoenicians," and, in the east part of the Middle East, as the "Mobeds." The leading center of these forces at that time was the Phoenician city of Tyre. In addition to the pact with King Philip, these forces controlled the Cult of Apollo at Delphi and Delos, the Greek state of Thebes, and owned leading factions in both Sparta and Athens in the same manner as Lord Shelburne owned the British Parliament of 1784.

The plan was concocted for a variety of intersecting reasons. First, despite bribery, despite the Peloponnesian War, and so forth, the Persian Empire could never conquer mainland Greece; Persian methods were no match for the Greek military system. Additionally, the fringes of the Persian Empire were becoming highly unstable, the satrapies were in an endemic state of revolt. The reasons were numerous; a detailed discussion of the matter is not relevant to the purposes of the discussion of the matter here.

What is relevant, is, first, that the plot was defeated by the victories of Alexander the Great, and, second, that the assassination of Alexander, by Aristotle et al., prevented Alexander from completing the program outlined in what is called his "Testament." It was the premature death of Alexander which made possible the creation of the Roman Empire, if approximately three centuries later.

On the eve of King Philip's march to implement the terms of the agreement, he was conveniently assassinated, and with the backing of the Academy at Athens, and the support of the Cyrenaic temple of Ammon, Alexander seized power, and destroyed the city of Tyre and the entirety of the Persian Empire. Despite the assassination of Alexander, his campaigns had so wrecked the institutions of the Persian Empire that it was approximately 250 years before the Chaldeans could put together another operation like the Western Division project.

The Chaldean model of oligarchical "empire" crops up repeatedly in history. It is older than Babylon. Politically, it is a collection of local, impotent, semi-autonomous political entities, each distinguished by some special ethnic, religious or ethnic-plus-religious feature. Usually, regional collections of such local, culturally semi-autonomous entities are grouped into an overlordship resembling a Persian imperial satrapy. One "nationality," such as the Assyrians, the Babylonians, the Medes, the Persians, the Phoenicians, or the Romans, squats on top of the entire heap, exerting military overlordship. In reality, the entire process is controlled from behind the scenes by syndicates of "families" of the Chaldean, or "Phoenician" type, "families" which are, on the one side rentier-financier "families" on the "Venetian model," and at the same time the families controlling the priesthood.

There Are No Limits to Growth

This was the form of the Persian Empire, the Roman Empire, the Byzantine Empire, the Ottoman Empire, the Austro-Hungarian Empire, and the Russian Empire.

From Charlemagne through the Emperor Frederick (Hohenstaufen) II, the Augustinian currents of Western European Christendom attempted to cope with the threat to civilization from Byzantium by taking over the authority of the old Roman Empire, and imbuing that imperial authority with the cultural matrix of St. Augustine's version of the Nicene Creed. The rise of the Inquisition, beginning A.D. 1230-1233, and the death of Frederick II, in A.D. 1250, led to a collapse of Charlemagne's design. By A.D. 1268, the Staufer had been wiped out in Italy and Spain, in the defeat of the Ghibelline (German: Waibling) faction (the Staufer) by the Venetian-led Guelph (German: Welf). In Italy, a resistance erupted, in the form of the White Guelph, republican faction, against the Black Guelph, oligarchical faction. The Black Guelph (called today the "black nobility") won, and the *fondi* of Italy, typified by Lombard banking houses such as the Bardi and Peruzzi, looted defeated Europe with usury.

Dante Alighieri, a political leader of the White Guelph faction, and ally of the Staufer, created a vast design for a new political order in Europe, to replace the imperial form of Charlemagne, the Saliers, and the Staufer. The center of the design was an Augustinian neo-Platonic order, defined by Dante's famous *Commedia*. The principles elaborated in the *Commedia* were not new in themselves; they had been the central features of Plato's policy, and St. Augustine's. What was new was Dante's treatment of the Italian language, and his design for a system of nation-states, implicit in his *De Monarchia*.

Contrary to a myth concocted by the Jesuits during the early nineteenth century, Italian is not a language descended from Latin. They are two quite distinct languages, although with a significant influence upon one another over two thousand years. The Latins of Rome conquered an Italian-speaking people, who remained the majority of the population of Italy, as is reflected in the fact that French and Spanish are predominantly versions of Italian, not Latin--as contrasted with New High German, a partly synthetic language, which is much more Latinized than any Romance language.

Dante did not object to Latin as such. The brutish Latin of the native Romans had been civilized by Hellenic influences, and the medieval Church, prior to the middle thirteenth century, had produced an elegant and sometimes profound literature in that improved language. The problem was, that the use of Latin as the common language of administration of an empire had encouraged the degradation of local forms of native languages into brutish dialects, to the effect that most of the population lacked the means to communicate important conceptions of policy in a rigorous form of discourse. Italian, Dante demonstrated, was at root a powerful language, in which not only elegance but great profundity could be expressed; he produced an Italian which is unmatched in beauty and power for communication to the present day. It was through organized public recitations of passages from the Commedia, notably during the fifteenth century, that the Italian population learned to speak and to think in Italian.

To achieve a true republic, in which the individual adult was capable of assuming the functions of a citizen, to deliberate in common the most profound issues of state policy, it was necessary that the citizens of a republic share a common form of literate language. Therefore, people who shared a common, literate language, and the philosophical outlook of republicanism, should form sovereign nation-state republics based on that literate form of language.

There Are No Limits to Growth

Dante's writings became the foundations of a far-flung conspiracy, which spread even during the darkest depths of the fourteenth century. Petrarch was recruited to this conspiracy, and became its leader, from his headquarters at Avignon. The rise of Augustinian teaching-orders, such as Groote's Brothers of the Common Life, promoted the renaissance which began to take shape during the late fourteenth century, capped, so to speak, by Brunelleschi's solution to the task of completing the dome on the Cathedral at Florence. Cardinal Nicholas of Cusa, who lifted the shattered Papacy from the rubble, and ultimately brought his collaborator Piccolomini to the Papacy as Pius II, perfected what Dante had begun. Beginning with his *Concordantia Catholica*, Cusa completed the design of the principles of law for nation-states, and for relations among sovereign nation-states, and also set into motion the revolution in mathematical physics which has dominated the past five hundred years of European civilization.

In the midst of this, Cusa led an effort to defeat the forces of Venice and Byzantium for once and for all, the famous 1439 Council of Florence, at which the Paleologues of Constantinople and circles including Cosimo de Medici, Cusa, and Cardinal Bessarion attempted to establish St. Augustine's principle of the Filioque as the common, ecumenical principle of the Western and Eastern Church. It nearly succeeded.

This may seem ancient history, but this part of history is the conscious determinant of the policy of the forces behind Bertrand Russell and his world-government project, and therefore indispensable for understanding why they have done as they have done over the course of the recent thirty-eight years.

By the middle of the fifteenth century, the *fondi* of the black nobility had significantly recovered from the wave of bankruptcies of great Lombard banking houses such as the

Bertrand Russell's Dream of World Empire

Bardi and Peruzzi during the middle of the previous century. They fought back against the Council of Florence, and in doing so, won a decisive battle, which re-established their continuing power in Europe to the present date. That battle was the fall of Constantinople in A.D. 1453.

The plot to destroy the power of the Paleologues in Constantinople was directed by Venice, and conducted in collaboration with the Genoese, old families of Rome whose family histories traced back to the Caesars, and the section of the Byzantine Church coordinated from Mount Athos. Venice entered into a pact with the Ottoman Turks to destroy the Paleologues, giving the Ottomans control over Constantinople and much of the remains of Byzantium as well. Gennadios, a spokesman for Mount Athos, used the Byzantine Church to command Greeks not to rally to the defense of Constantinople. The Venetians and Roman families supplied the Ottomans with artillery, and gunners. Four thousand Genoese mercenaries, hired to assist in the defense of Constantinople, overpowered the guards at the-walls and gates by night, and admitted the Ottoman troops to conquer and loot the city.

In return, the Ottoman ruler, Mohammed the Conqueror, gave Gennadios, soon become Patriarch, control over the affairs of non-Islamic populations within the Ottoman domain. Venice was given a substantial part of the conquered Greek regions, and also given the powerful position of *dragoman*, in fact the Ottoman intelligence and diplomatic services. Venice created and controlled the Ottoman Empire *from the inside*.

During the same period, with the rise of Isabella and Ferdinand in Spain, Genoa took over Isabella, and most of the Iberian peninsula, despite continued resistance from Ferdinand as long as he lived. With the Italian Golden Renaissance's ally, the Paleologues, destroyed in the East, and with use of Spanish infantry from the West, the

Venetians waged an ultimately winning battle against the Golden Renaissance in Italy itself, gaining control of Italy with the death of Cesare Borgia, the military leader who had been Leonardo da Vinci's last card in his effort to save Italy.

During the same period, Venice took over Bavaria and began building up the future Austro-Hungarian Empire, to serve as a check against the advances of the Ottoman Empire. Venice controlled both the Habsburgs and the Ottomans from the inside, and controlled both by aid of playing the one creation against the other. This Balkan game continued into World War I, when Venice, then under the leadership of Count Volpi di Misurata, completed its long plan for the destruction of both empires, and the Russian Empire and Germany as well. Then, V. I. Lenin, sent into Russia as a supposed Venetian asset, by Venetian agent Alexander Helphand (Parvus), outwitted the Venetians with his October 1917 Revolution, and by retaining Bolshevik power, created a circumstance in Russia which prompted the Venetians to play the same game of World War I over again, in only slightly altered form, as World War II.

Meanwhile, Venice's schemes received a decisive setback during the second half of the fifteenth century, with the creation of the first modern form of sovereign nation-state by France's King Louis XI. The success of Louis XI created the circumstances in which the faction known to history as the English Erasmians, as typified in history by Sir Thomas More, created the second sovereign nation-state in civil war-ruined England. The destruction of these two sovereign nation-states became the object of Venice and Genoa over the period from then through the 1815 Congress of Vienna. England was conquered in 1603, and regained by Genoa in 1660. France was not destroyed by the 1815 Treaty of Vienna, but it was weakened internally to the point it never resumed its former power. The key to this operation was a marriage between the Burgundian house of Charles the Bold and the Habsburgs, which produced, in due course, the future Habsburg Emperor Charles V.

Venice's organization of the German peasant war, and butchery of the peasantry, in 1525-26, its orchestration of the process of Reformation in Germany, Charles V's control of the Spanish throne, and the Habsburg sack of Rome, on behalf of Venice, in A.D. 1527, gave Venice power over all of Europe except France and England. The Papacy of Cusa and Pius II was crushed, Venice organized the Counter Reformation, using the Jesuits and other features of the Hospitaller order as leading instruments. A nightmare, a new dark age, descended upon most of Europe until the Pope's trusted agent, Cardinal Mazarin, organized the breaking of the power of the Spanish Habsburgs in A.D. 1653.

To understand the Counter Reformation, one must see its essential features. It was a campaign to destroy and eradicate everything which Cardinal Nicholas of Cusa and the fifteenth-century Papacy had achieved: the sovereign nation-state, the Cusan doctrine of natural law and the currents of scientific method associated with it, and Augustinian (neo-Platonic) theology. The intellectual weapons of the Counter Reformation were chiefly Aristotle and Roman imperial law.

This was the Venetian cultural matrix imposed upon Britain. During the eighteenth century, the long-range policy discussions among leading circles in Britain were pivoted on questions of Roman imperial law and history. Gibbon's treatment is merely best-known among these studies. During the nineteenth century, Venice's influence over the Acton family, and the important Bulwer-Lytton, led into the Oxford circles of Benjamin Jowett and John

There Are No Limits to Growth

Ruskin, and the formation of the Pre-Raphaelite Brotherhood. The Fabian Society, British (guild) socialism, and Lord Alfred Milner's Coefficients, Round Table, and Chatham House, were concentrated expressions of this process. Bertrand Russell, grandson of Prime Minister Lord John Russell and godson of John Stuart Mill, was a concentrated expression of this viewpoint developed over the course of the nineteenth century.

Russell himself displayed the peculiar twist of his thinking in the manner he walked out of Milner's Coefficient circles in 1902. At the point he walked out of that restaurant meeting, the trend of discussion was the need to prepare for the inevitable general war ahead. British industry was in no condition for such an impending conflict. The British navy was obsolete and chiefly sinkable. The army was still using musket-fire volley tactics. And so on. An industrial mobilizaton and retooling of the military forces were deemed imperative.

Russell never had an objection to war as such. A few samplings of his views on the subject are probably indispensable at this point.

In 1951, he wrote:

> But bad times, you say, are exceptional, and can be dealt with by exceptional methods. This has been more or less true during the honeymoon period of industrialism, but it will not remain true unless *the increase of population can be enormously diminished*. . . . War, so far, has had no very great effect on this increase, . . .*War*. . *.has hitherto been disappointing in this respect.* . . . *but perhaps bacteriological war may prove more effective. If a Black Death could spread throughout the world once in every generation*, the survivors

Bertrand Russell's Dream of World Empire

could procreate freely without making the world too full. . . . The state of affairs might be somewhat unpleasant, but what of it? Really high-minded people are indifferent to happiness, especially other people's [emphasis added—L.H.L.].

In 1927, H. G. Wells, World War I chief of British foreign-intelligence, wrote a proposal for an "Open Conspiracy," in which he summed up his proposals as follows:

1. The complete assertion, practical as well as theoretical, of the provisional nature of existing governments and of our acquiescence to them;
2. The resolve to minimize by all available means the conflicts of these governments, their militant use of individuals and property and their interferences with the establishment of a world economic system;
3. The determination to replace private local or national ownership of at least credit, transport, and staple production by a responsible world directorate serving the common ends of the race;
4. The practical recognition of the necessity for world biological controls, for example, of population and disease;
5. The support of a minimum standard of individual freedom and welfare in the world;
6. The supreme duty of subordinating the personal life to the creation of a world directorate capable of these tasks and to the general advancement of human knowledge, capacity, and power.

There Are No Limits to Growth

To which Russell replied: "I do not know of anything with which I agree more entirely."

From the same general period, Russell made the following observations, which bear upon his interpretation of Wells's "Open Conspiracy" manifesto:

> Socialism, especially international socialism, is only possible as a stable system if the population is stationary or nearly so. A slow increase might be coped with by improvements in agricultural methods, but a rapid increase must in the end reduce the whole population to penury . . . *the white population of the world will soon cease to increase.* The Asiatic races will be longer, and the negroes still longer, before their birth rate falls sufficiently to make their numbers stable without help of war and pestilence. . . . Until that happens, the benefits aimed at by socialism can only be partially realized, and *the less prolific races will have to defend themselves against the more prolific by methods which are disgusting even if they are necessary* [emphasis added--L.H.L].

Russell walked out of the Milner Coefficients not because they prepared for war, but because they proposed to use industrial build-up to save a system of nation-states. Hence, Russell was not inconsistent in proposing nuclear war during his campaign for world-government at the close of World War II. His pacifism of the World War I period, his role, in concert with fellows such as Aldous Huxley, in establishing the Peace Pledge Union of the 1930s, and his supposed pacifism of the 1950s and 1960s, are consistent expressions of Russell s policy: a world-government ruled by the Anglo-Saxon race, and possessed of a monopoly of the means to employ methods which are disgusting even if

Bertrand Russell's Dream of World Empire

they are' necessary. Russell s consistent policy was his goal of "socialism," of Malthusian world-government dedicated to reducing the populations of the darker-skinned populations by "methods which are disgusting even if they are necessary."

Many shared Russell's general views over the past thirty-eight year period--and longer. This agreement was the foundation of the World Association of Parliamentarians for World Government, and the process of "back-channel" negotiations known as the Pugwash Conferences.

It happened that the growth of the Soviet nuclear and thermonuclear arsenals delimited the possible negotiations of world-government with the Soviet leadership, to proposals for what were in effect at least two "empires," and possibly three. Not that the fellows who conducted such negotiations actually intended to live side by side with a Russian-ruled "Eastern Division" of the new Persian Empire. After all, one may always hope to cheat on agreements. This point has been stressed recently by Henry A. Kissinger's former mentor and present business partner, Lord Peter Carrington. Carrington, while proposing a "New Yalta" pact with the Soviet government, and proclaiming that present Soviet General Secretary Yuri Andropov is a precious Soviet asset of Carrington's foreign policy, also assured the public that he is maintaining a "death watch" over the Soviet Union. What Lord Peter signifies by "death watch" is by no means a dark secret. It has been the generally stated view of fellows such as Kissinger, Zbigniew Brzezinski, and many others of the same general orbit, that the "Soviet Empire" is near the brink of eruption of waves of ethnic and religious insurgences, projected to sweep from the Comecon states of Eastern Europe, through the Soviet Ukraine, and the Caucasus, into the Islamic populations of Central Asia.

As to the Soviet KGB's knowledge of Lord Peter's thinking in the matter, we shall come to that in due course here. The immediate working point is that the Eastern Establishment of the United States has been willing to destroy the economies of the United States, Western Europe, and the developing nations, on the basis of the assumption that the "Soviet Empire" will crumble from within before the point of weakness of the West is reached at which the Soviets might be able to exploit the growing weakness of the economies and military capabilities of the West. Since the transition period of 1964-68, that Eastern Establishment, and its confederates in Western Europe, have been most successfully destroying the West from within.

We shall examine that process of destruction of the West next, and after that, turn our attention to the problems posed by Soviet Secretary Andropov and company in this connection.

The Malthusian Logic of Nuclear Deterrence

From the beginning of its implementation, during the early 1960s, the strategic doctrine of Nuclear Deterrence has depended upon the condition that neither superpower develop adequate means for destroying thermonuclear ballistic missiles in flight, before such launched missiles could explode against their targets. For that reason, Henry A. Kissinger's successful negotiation of a treaty limiting deployment of anti-ballistic missile *defensive systems*, during 1972, fulfilled a fundamental objective of the forces sponsoring the Pugwash Conference. It is this attempt to prevent the development of anti-missile defensive systems which is the heart of the Nuclear Deterrence doctrine, as Deterrence was defined by Szilard in his 1958 Pugwash address.

Bertrand Russell's Dream of World Empire

If efficient anti-ballistic missile (ABM) defensive systems are developed, which means, chiefly, ABM systems based on lasers and related kinds of directed beams, it is potentially the case that such systems would not only be extremely efficient, but that the cost of destroying a thermonuclear ballistic missile in flight would become cheaper, by an order of magnitude, perhaps, than building and launching such a missile. In that case, if two powers are more or less matched in economic potential, the power which relies on the defensive system can destroy almost totally the missile launch of the attacking power, after which the attacking power becomes virtually helpless against the defending power. Today, for example, both the United States and Soviet Union are within the range of more or less five years' distance from the possibility of deploying ABM systems which could assuredly destroy up to 99 percent or more of the ballistic missiles launched by the other. In that case, thermonuclear ballistic missiles become obsolete, and the whole point of Szilard's design of Nuclear Deterrence is out the window forever.

However, if Pugwash could manipulate both superpowers into banning development of anything but very limited ABM systems, such that perhaps 50 percent or more of the thermonuclear missiles launched destroy their targets, in this case thermonuclear missiles have the practical effect of being an ultimate weapon. In this case, the spokesmen for Nuclear Deterrence argue, any superpower which might launch a general war would be struck by a thermonuclear bombardment by the opposing superpower. This, the argument runs, means that both superpowers would be more or less completely ruined by such a war. In other words, "Mutual and Assured Destruction," or MAD.

In the West, the spokesmen for MAD, or Nuclear Deterrence, argue that the first, and possibly second salvo

77

of thermonuclear missiles would mean such destruction of both powers that neither would possess the economic resources to conduct general warfare beyond the point of those barrages. Therefore, they continued their thinking on this matter, *there really is no point in maintaining the kind of military establishment of the sort which would be used only after the initial thermonuclear missile barrages.* Therefore, they continued their argument, *there is no longer any military reason for keeping the kind of technologically progressive and growing economy which would be required to support a full-scale "conventional" military capability.* As long as the economic-technological basis is sufficient to support the needed Nuclear Deterrent, it will be enough to let the economies stagnate technologically, even to let them collapse to the levels at which "conventional" military forces are sufficient merely for fighting "local," colonial-style warfare.

This has been the strategic doctrine followed since Lyndon B. Johnson became President of the United States, the doctrine of McGeorge Bundy, Robert S. McNamara, Henry Kissinger, among others. Granted, these Pugwashed spokesmen for the Eastern Establishment were obliged to proceed with some caution at first. Traditional military professionals balked as much as their professional code permitted; the general public was not ready to swallow a massive dose of takedown of defense capabilities and the economy as well, at least not abruptly. Over the period 1964-68, with the growing unpopularity of the U.S. military, because of the protracted war in Vietnam, public opinion acquiesced substantially. By 1972-73, and the consolidation of "détente" with the Soviet Union, what Szilard outlined in 1958 was already established as prevailing policy and practice, if with a few minor adjustments in the policy over the intervening years.

By the time McGeorge Bundy was promoted from chief

of Johnson's National Security Council, to President of the Ford Foundation, in 1966, the topmost ranks of government were already locked into both a Nuclear Deterrence policy and a neo-Malthusian policy, a policy of transforming the United States into a "post-industrial society." The first major step in the direction of a "post-industrial society" was taken with Johnson's "Great Society" package-policy of the middle 1960s. The background, briefly, was as follows.

Approximately 1927, Bertrand Russell presented his proposal for a three-point transformation of society generally. The first was the policy that all fundamental scientific progress be halted. The second proposed the development of inexpensive methods of mass-drugging of populations, as a measure of social control. The third was a proposal to reverse the language revolution set into motion by Dante Alighieri, to destroy those features of language-in-use which make possible rigorous communication upon important questions of policy among populations generally.

During 1938, after assembling the Peace Pledge Union in Britain, Russell and his collaborator Aldous Huxley made new visits to the United States. Aldous Huxley returned to California, where he resumed his earlier work promoting the use of marijuana and proliferation of hesychastic pagan cults. Russell established a deep collaboration with Chicago University's President Robert Hutchins. Russell and Hutchins collaborated to launch a project known as the Unification of the Sciences, in collaboration with such figures as the American Museum of Natural History's Margaret Mead and her husband of that period, Gregory Bateson. Into this effort were drawn Russell's old Fabian collaborator from the World War I period, Germany's Karl Korsch, brainwasher Dr. Kurt Lewin, radical positivist Rudolf Carnap, a Korsch collaborator since the early 1930s, and sundry others.

Language-destroying versions of "linguistics" were introduced to the University of Pennsylvania. However, it would not be until after World War II, that the fuller effect of this project was experienced in the United States.

During the war, a Swiss laboratory developed a synthetic version of the drug ergotamine, called LSD-25. This was a drug of the category called psychotomimetic, because of the produced symptoms of paranoid schizophrenic psychosis in the user. Aldous Huxley headed off from Tavistock in London to California, where he teamed with Gregory Bateson and others in a project called "MK-Ultra." This project, which was centered in Palo Alto, California, headquarters of the RAND Corporation and the Stanford Research Institute, was an experimental pilot program in both the use of psychotropic drugs, including LSD-25, and the usefulness of such drugs and their after effects in catalyzing the creation of religious and other cults.

Both the RAND Corporation and Stanford Research Institute have notable pedigrees. RAND was a spin-off of the war-time Strategic Bombing Survey, a creation of the psychological warfare center of the British secret intelligence service, the London Tavistock Clinic of Brigadier Dr. John Rawlings Rees and Dr. Eric Trist. Not only was RAND a spawn of this Strategic Bombing Survey, but top-ranking officials of the post-war London Tavistock Institute directly supervised RAND's early period. Stanford Research Institute, also of Tavistock pedigree, has become the center for promoting projects based on H. G. Wells's "Open Conspiracy" manifesto of 1927.

This project in California was interfaced with the network of institutions associated with Dr. Kurt Lewin, including the Lewin center at the Massachusetts Institute of Technology (MIT), the University of Michigan, and the National Training Laboratories, the latter the coordinator of the National Education Association, a teachers' association. The operations at the Lewinite center at MIT include a RAND project directed by Dr. Alex Bavelas, and the presence of Professor Noam Chomsky, a political associate of Karl Korsch, and product of the Russell linguistics program at the University of Pennsylvania. Key coordination for these projects was provided through the Josiah Macy, Jr., Foundation, a creation of a branch of the Quaker Macy family of department store fame, an institution which featured such figures as Gregory Bateson and Margaret Mead. Chomsky's work at MIT included collaboration with a project directed by Professor Marvin Minsky, a program in so-called "artificial intelligence" simulations by computer: Chomsky-Minsky programs efficiently simulate human psychosis on computers.

By 1963, the pilot programs associated with projects such as MK-Ultra became operational programs. The Ukiah Valley in California was opened up for experimental cults, including the subsequently notorious Peoples' Temple of the Reverend Jim Jones. Millions of doses of LSD-25 were distributed among witting and unwitting recipients on campuses around the nation, while Tavistock's experimental Dionysian cult project, the Beatles, was introduced to the United States. The rock-drug counterculture was in full swing.

During 1964, Robert Hutchins, working out of a Ford Foundation-funded project, the Fund for the Republic, issued a proposal entitled the *Triple Revolution*, the model for Johnson's "Great Society" program. This proposed that "cybernation," automated machines, were creating such a rapid growth in productivity (3 percent per year at that time), that a growing mass of permanently unemployed was being amassed, especially among the so-called minority groups. The report proposed a new policy-paradigm for society, the shift from emphasis on investment in productive employment, to distribution of social services to the growing mass of production-useless poor.

Apart from the *Triple Revolution* report itself, it was leading policy during the early 1960s, that the United States was shifting from an "industrial economy" to a "services economy." With President Johnson's inauguration in January 1965, the new, Malthusian policy-paradigms were ready to erupt.

The final catalyst was a report on the social effects of the NASA "research and development program prepared and submitted by the London Tavistock Institute, the so-called "Rapaport Report." This report lamented the fact that the achievements of NASA research and development were inducing "excessive" technological optimism, and high regard for rational behavior generally within the population. This pro-science impact must be stopped and reversed. Johnson complied; a massive takedown of the U.S. aerospace research and development establishment began during 1966-67, diverting funds into "Great Society" projects, including "consumerism" and "environmentalism." The paradigm-shift from technological progress and economic growth, toward "post-industrial society," had occurred.

This intersected another leading social development of the period from about 1956-58 into the middle 1960s: the New Left projects coordinated chiefly, internationally, between the League for Industrial Democracy and the Socialist International, producing such developments as SDS in West Germany and, later, SDS in the United States. The common denominator of this effort, from the U.S. side, was not only the British Fabian Society's old front organization, the League of Industrial Democracy (LID), but also the 1930s-1940s apparatus of Sidney Hillman and David Dubinsky, the latter the ruler of the International Ladies Garment Workers' Union (ILGWU), the post-war

Bertrand Russell's Dream of World Empire

base of operations for Jay Lovestone, In Europe, this same apparatus was represented by Paris-Switzerland-based Irving Brown of the AFL-CIO's international department. Through this international network, a collection of "old lefties" of the early to middle 1950s were mustered to apply their skills to creating a non-Marxist variety of youth radicalism, initially with a credible dosage of either Marxist or seeming-Marxist verbiage and posturing. Essentially, it was an existentialist movement, a blend of Jean-Paul Sartre and the London Tavistock Clinic's R. D. Laing.

In the United States' case, this was begun as a "regroupment" of small circles and grouplets of Trotskyist, Communist, and Third Camp varieties of relics from the 1930s and 1940s, in the wake of, first, Nikita Khrushchev's Twentieth Congress denunciation of Stalin, and the beginnings of a visible Moscow-Peking rift. This collection was marched, beginning 1958, into and through the civil rights ferment, into the black power movements of the early 1960s, and into the anti-war movement launched by leading circles of the Eastern Establishment at the close of 1964. In France, West Germany, Italy, and so forth, the early phases were parallel but different in detail. With the emergence of the anti-war ferment, they converged, and converged upon the coordinated eruptions of 1968.

By 1968, the preconditions for Kissinger's arrival had ripened. What had been launched as pilot programs by Johnson's administration was escalated into full-scale operations under Kissinger. Malthusianism was made the official policy of NATO. The NATO "strategy of tension" was unleashed, coordinated with the eruption of terrorism in West Germany, Italy, and the United States, in 1969. At the close of 1969, the "environmentalist" movements were launched top-down, simultaneously in the United States and Europe. During 1969, a top-down organization of the beginnings of proselytizing mass movements of recruitment to male homosexuality and lesbianism were unleashed, with the newly-created "Women's Liberation Movement" the principal vehicle for the spread of lesbian cults manufactured by prolonged, degrading "sensitivity sessions."

That is how it happened. It all happened through a coordinated, top-down paradigm-shift in policies of governments and in mass behavior and radically shifted popular values in the populations generally. *It was a general cultural paradigm-shift*, a shift toward the values which Bertrand Russell esteemed so much, a shift accomplished by "methods which are disgusting even if they are necessary."

"The Third and Final Roman Empire"

It may be an exaggeration, but only an exaggeration, that today, there are more actively professing Marxists in and around the universities of the "Western" nations, than are presently to be found in the nations of the Soviet Bloc. Approximately the middle of the 1960s, the drift away from Marxist thinking, if not Marxist terminology, which had become prominent in Eastern Europe since about 1956, became the visible trend even among leading circles in the Soviet Union itself. Today, Soviet officials are usually classed as "Soviet pragmatists," and even in the Soviet Union, the churches are not merely filled, but overflowing.

It takes almost no imagination to recognize that some leading anti-Soviet figures are enormously pleased by the shift from Marxism to pragmatism and religion in the Comecon nations. Mr. Henry A. Kissinger professes to be very pleased. So does his business partner, Lord Peter Carrington. So does the man who Kissinger replaced at Harvard University, and who replaced Kissinger as chief of the U.S. National Security Council, Zbigniew Brzezinski.

Bertrand Russell's Dream of World Empire

Mr. Brzezinski himself is a man blessed with an enormous and seemingly inexhaustible imagination in matters bearing upon Eastern Europe and Asia. All of us have a neighbor or other acquaintance of similar talent: the neighbor, for example, who, on almost any occasion, can promptly invent a fact which the universe as a whole could never otherwise produce. In brief, Mr. Brzezinski is broadly typical of those policy influencers in the West who have a very devout wish that the Soviet Empire destroy itself from within, and who select purely from their imagination any beliefs which may be needed to assure themselves their wish is within arm's reach of being fulfilled. It is not the case of Mr. Brzezinski which we wish to emphasize here, but rather what he typifies insofar as he typifies anything at all.

Is the Soviet Empire near the beginning of its internal destruction, as fellows of Mr. Brzezinski's persuasion insist? Or, have such fellows ignored some most important facts concerning the cultures of many among the Slavic and Islamic populations of that empire? Not only have they overlooked such important facts, but these facts were readily available to them from leading circles in the Church of England, leading cultural research institutions of Venice, or from learned circles among the monasteries at Mount Athos in Greece. Moreover, since the late fifteenth century, there has been accumulated a vast literature documenting the facts Brzezinski et al. have overlooked, as well as new, scholarly studies currently in circulation as books, or proceedings of conferences recently held in Rome.

On what we say on this subject now, the accuracy and importance of the facts we employ are acknowledged among the varieties of experts we indicated, and at the highest rank of the most learned, and currently best-informed on the situation inside the Soviet Union itself. All these facts, fellows of Brzezinski's official position and concern might have possessed easily, had they not wishfully avoided such well-known experts. As to the conclusion we draw from these facts, the experts generally agree that this writer's evaluation is not merely "possibly correct," but agree that, at worst, this writer's evaluation is the only hypothesis worth study and debate at this time.

So far, in both this present chapter and the preceding one, we have examined the roots of Malthusianism in the West in terms of what we have identified as "cultural paradigms." The Calvinist thesis we quoted from Adam Smith's 1759 *Theory of Moral Sentiments*, is an example of a cultural paradigm, or at least the kernel of such a paradigm. The cultural paradigm of the Essex Junto families of New England, and of the U.S. Eastern Establishment of today, is another example. The shift from emphasis on technological progress to "environmentalism" and "post-industrial society" is a dramatic shift in dominant cultural paradigm of the U.S.A. and Western Europe, which most among us have experienced directly during our own lifetimes. Now, our attention is directed to the phenomenon of Soviet Malthusianism, a rapidly growing influence within the Soviet leadership and the hierarchy of the Russian Orthodox Church. The influential Soviet KGB official, Patriarch Pimen of the Russian Orthodox Church, is an example of this, perhaps even more a neo-Malthusian fanatic than Ivan Frolov and others associated with the Soviet Global Systems Analysis apparatus.

What we have to say on the internal cultural developments within the Soviet Empire today should be compared with the writings of Dr. Armin Mohler, spokesman for the Bavarian Siemens Stiftung. Dr. Mohler, earlier a Swiss volunteer in Adolf Hitler's Waffen-SS, completed his studies during the immediate post-war period under Swiss Nazi-sympathizer Karl Jaspers, producing a dissertation in 1949, subsequently published, in 1950 and later editions, under the title *The Conservative Revolution*. Although the book is usually viewed as an apology for the Nazis, and for the "new right" of today, it is much more important than that. It is one of the most detailed, and largely accurate maps of the mental processes which produce a Nazi. Once one understands that mental map of the Nazi mind, one is able to predict more or less accurately what a Nazi would do, what his goals are, how those goals will shift somewhat as a Nazi movement matures, and so forth and so on. What Dr. Mohler describes as the cultural shifts among European nineteenth-century currents, leading into the emergence of twentieth-century fascism generally, and Nazism in particular, is most similar to what is occurring in the Soviet Empire today. It is more or less sufficient to substitute the Russian novelist Dostoevsky, for the German-language Swiss, Friedrich Nietzsche.

This is something more substantial than merely a comparison. The Soviet KGB of today is in close and massive collaboration with a wealthy and powerful, global, centrally coordinated network most accurately described as the "Nazi international." This organization was assembled by combined efforts of certain Western intelligence services, which wished to employ elements of the Nazi apparatus, especially Amt VI of the Nazi RSHA, as a post-war anti-Soviet capability. In return, the Soviet state security apparatus had deep penetration and control of the same networks, and used it against the West. At the same time, the Nazi international reassembled over the period 1943-1950 was backed and controlled by powerful Swiss bankers who continued to be fanatically Nazi even after the war. International terrorism is almost entirely created and coordinated through this Nazi international. It is the dominant organized force within the Islamic "fundamentalist," or Sufi movements of the Islamic world, and the leading force active within the various secular forms of "integrist" ("separatist") movements of India, the

Middle East, Western Europe, and so forth today. It overlaps the Sufi Freemasonic networks of Europe and the U.S.A., and is a dominant force within a far-flung organization called Islam and the West, as well as within the Malthusian Club of Rome.

Self-styled "right-wingers" of the West, including some of high rank within or relative to official intelligence agencies, persist in confidence that this Nazi international is their asset and ally against the Soviet Empire. Certain nominal liberals of the West, of similar positions, consider the Nazi international and its adjuncts a matter of anti-Soviet "methods which are disgusting even if they are necessary." They blind themselves to facts which should begin to be made apparent to them if they compared the implications of Dr. Mohler's *Conservative Revolution* with the special sort of predominantly fascistic tendencies erupting within the Soviet command and certain associated social currents of the Soviet Empire's populations. The emergence of Soviet Malthusianism is merely an included feature of this trend within the command and populations of the Soviet Empire, but it is one among the crucial pieces of diagnostic evidence prominently to be considered in this connection.

Apart from all the faults of Dr. Karl Marx, he was an impassioned anti-Malthusian.

He was situated, together with his associate, Frederick Engels, within the British currents identified, earlier, during the 1820s and 1830s, with the famous automatic calculating machine designer, Charles Babbage, and with the Edinburgh and Cambridge circles allied with Babbage, whose efforts produced the British Association for the Advancement of Science (BAAS), and BAAS's U.S. branch, AAAS. The BAAS circles were not philosophically anti-Malthusian, but they did argue that the Malthusians of Oxford University, of the London Royal

Society, and Haileybury, had gone much too far in holding back study of science and progress in technology. Much like the majority among Milner's Coefficients at the beginning of the present century, they argued that Britain was strategically imperiled by the fact that British science was far behind that in the U.S.A. and the continent of Europe generally, and also falling dangerously behind the pace of technological progress on the continent of Europe. For such reasons these gentlemen, including the Cambridge Apostles' circles to which Engels was connected by family business affairs and in related ways, made an entirely artificial distinction between the political-economic doctrines of Adam Smith and David Ricardo, on the one side, and the overt anti-technology fanaticism of Malthus et al.

Karl Marx himself came under the strong influence of Engels on these points during the middle 1840s, and, while in London, came under the supervision of a leading intelligence operative of Lord Palmerston's SIS, David Urquhart of the British Museum. The essential character of Urquhart's circles is underlined by the case of Dr. Edward Aveling. Aveling, at one point in his life the lover of the Blavatskian theosophical leader Annie Besant, was steered to one of Marx's daughters working with Marx in the British Museum, and married her. This Aveling, who is on surviving records of the matter, an all-around scoundrel, was responsible for attributing to Marx's first edition of *Capital I* a dedication to Charles Darwin, a man whom Marx despised as a Malthusian, and Aveling became associated with the John Ruskin circles, including the Hammersmith Society. Nonetheless, during the 1840s and 1850s, Marx's views were those of the Babbage variety of British anti-Malthusians, and remained emphatically so throughout the remainder of his life and writings.

It was for approximately a century and longer, one of

the leading arguments against capitalism, by Marx and the Marxists, that capitalism braked technological progress, and that this braking caused great harm to the world's population generally. The same viewpoint was strongly professed by V. I. Lenin, whose commitment to the technological-industrial development of Soviet Russia may have differed in form, but not general direction, from the earlier "westernizers," such as Czars Peter I and Alexander II, or Sergei Count Witte at the turn of the century. One may also recall the Soviet "industrialization debates" of the 1920s, the Five Year Plans of the Stalin period, sputnik, and so on.

It is therefore rather stunning, at first notice of the fact, to find the son-in-law of former Soviet industrializer A. Kosygin, Dzerhman Gvishiani, to have been Lord Solly Zuckerman's predecessor as head of the rabidly Malthusian International Institute for Applied Systems Analysis (IIASA), or to read the rabidly Malthusian ravings of Ivan Frolov and his circles in leading official publications under control of the Soviet KGB. Or, one notices that on May 10, 1982, a top KGB official, Patriarch Pimen of the Russian Orthodox Church, devoted his keynote address to an international, Moscow peace conference, to a fanatical attack upon this writer's February 1982 announcement of a proposed new strategic doctrine for the United States, replacing MAD with parallel, U.S.A.-Soviet development and deployment of strategic ABM defense systems to end the age of thermonuclear terror. Pimen's argument was significant on account of other prominent features. His argument was that of a typical rabidly Malthusian Jesuit spokesman, an argument which both Pimen and the Jesuits, as well as rabidly Malthusian Franciscan spokesmen, copy directly from a falsified version of the Judeo-Christian Book of Genesis known as the "Gnostic Bible."

Pimen's doctrine of May 10, 1982 is interesting not only

Bertrand Russell's Dream of World Empire

because he devoted that keynote address to that degree to a personal attack upon this writer. The same formula erupted in a declaration issued by members of the Vatican's Pontifical Academy of Science, including such signators as the French geneticist, Professor Jéréme LeJeune, in September 1982, a month before Dr. Edward Teller's echoing of this writer's proposed strategic doctrine before an October 25, 1982 meeting of the Washington, D.C., National Press Club. So, the Jesuits of the Pontifical Academy were plainly attacking nothing but this writer's version of the proposed new strategic doctrine. Moreover, Professor LeJeune, who travelled with a group from the Pontifical Academy for high-level meetings with Soviet officials during 1982, followed the September 1982 statement by conducting a persisting and escalating campaign against this writer in France, the United States, and elsewhere, charging this writer with being a Soviet KGB "agent" on grounds of the same proposed strategic doctrine. Was this Professor LeJeune, ostensibly a right-wing Catholic with extremely right-wing views in genetics, actually an agent of the Soviet KGB?

Later, when President Ronald Reagan announced leading aspects of the writer's earlier proposed new U.S. strategic doctrine as official U.S. strategic doctrine, on March 23, 1983, the Soviet attack on Reagan's doctrine, from Secretary Yuri Andropov on down, was modeled exactly on Patriach Pimen's attack on this writer on May 10, 1982. The same Soviet KGB line was echoed by all associated with the Pugwash Conferences' policies worldwide.

All this was no accidental coincidence. On the Soviet side, these developments reflected an ongoing, and far-advanced paradigm-shift within leading circles of the Soviet Union. On the Western side, it reflected, in part, deep Soviet KGB collaboration with the Jesuits, Protestant circles of the Geneva-based.World Council of Churches, and deep Soviet collaboration with the Switzerland-based Nazi international.

The close interface between the Jesuit order's leadership and the Soviet KGB is fully documented. The connection dates from the Venetian families' deep connections into Russia and the Russian Orthodox Church hierarchy, and includes the Jesuits' decades-long residence in Russia during the period the order was banned by the Papacy during the eighteenth and early nineteenth centuries. The connection is maintained, in part, through the Jesuit church in Russia, the so-called "Byzantine Rite" or "Uniates," which also serves as an important Soviet KGB link into as far west as the United States. The "solidarist" network bridging East and West is a joint operation of the Jesuits and the Orthodox church's hierarchy, including the Soviet KGB's Russian Orthodox Church, a link actively maintained for important day-to-day matters through Vienna, and including such forces as the German and other anthroposophs as part of the "pagan" supporting apparatus.

However, although this connection is well known to all upper echelons of Western intelligence services--some of whom participate in these operations--the consoling View is maintained in such circles, that this constitutes a successful, and massive penetration of the East by the West. The overwhelming burden of the evidence is evidence that this estimate of the KGB-Jesuit connection is entirely mistaken. These intelligence services are, chiefly, ingenuously blind to the true character of Venice, Switzerland, the Jesuit order, and the cultural matrix of Byzantine forms of Slavic cultures. These gentlemen are relying on contemporary Western mass media culture, in which nothing is "credible" unless it is circulated wrapped in highly-respected, nationally-advertised "brand labels," with simple, easy-to-read instructions on the package.

Bertrand Russell's Dream of World Empire

The essence of the matter is this. It is well-known to upper echelons of Western intelligence services, that the prevailing strategic doctrine in very influential Soviet leading circles, is not Marxist-Leninist, or what might be described as "Soviet nationalist." The terms often used in these Soviet circles, according to some of the most highly-placed intelligence sources, is "The Third and Final Roman Empire," *the prophecy, dating from a famous letter of Philotheos of Pskov to Vasilij III (1503-1533), prophesying that the Russian Caesar (Czar), would rule over the third and final form of a Roman world-empire.* This letter was the basis for Ivan IV's adoption of first use of the title of Czar, and the basis upon which the Russian Orthodox Church thereafter insisted that all Rusian rulers adopt the title of Czar. *How is it possible, even barely conceivable, that modern, presumably atheistic Soviet leaders, would base the current strategy of the Soviet Union on a religious prophecy from the beginning of the sixteenth century?*

Obviously, if this picture of Soviet policy is accurate, the United States, and most so-called Western leaders generally, have an absurd view of the strategic problem represented by the Soviet Union today. Those leaders have overlooked the significance of the emergence of a growing current of Malthusianism within the Soviet leadership--and population. Is it, perhaps, simply the fact that those misguided leaders of the West have become so attached to the idea of "combating atheistic Communism," that they refuse to recognize the existence of any other, far more dangerous source of danger, simply to hold onto a truism from the past, a truism become largely a mere myth in the realities of today? Does not the accumulation of evidence, including such minor, but indicative matters as the LeJeune case, oblige us to reassess the matter of who is influencing whom through Pugwash Conference, Dartmouth Conference, and religious forms of East-West "back-channel" operations? *What if religion has become a*

93

leading instrument of Soviet strategic policy, and also state policy within the Comecon itself? Is this properly credible, actually provable fact? If so, how did this happen, and how does it work?

Suppose, that by exploiting the cultural resources of the Russian Church's Byzantine tradition, traditions deeply buried in the Slavic populations of the East, and by Soviet KGB collaboration with the Nazi international, to bring under control also Islamic insurgency, the "integrist" insurgencies inclusively erupting now in the East and along Soviet borders, are turned to Soviet advantage? Suppose also, that the Soviet leadership, by working closely with the Nazi international, is making itself the national homeland, so to speak, of a new kind of international, pro-Soviet mass movement, replacing the old, collapsing Communist International? Suppose that religious leaders in the West, themselves deeply affected by the Malthusian cultural paradigm-shift, are in a state they are rather easily manipulated by this new variety of Soviet international propaganda? Such questions fit the massive accumulation of corresponding varieties of fact, and fit them quite neatly. The conclusions are therefore, statistically speaking, the most probable explanations in sight. Yet, are they not only probable, but provably true?

Is world-rule by Soviet Czars, the end toward which the recent decades' rise of neo-Malthusianism is leading us? Is this the realization of the "international socialism" which Bertrand Russell proposed back during the 1920s, and which he attempted to bring into being beginning his contribution to the October 1946 issue of the *Bulletin of the Atomic Scientists?*

From the vantage-point of what Russell proposed during the late 1940s, and what Leo Szilard proposed in his 1958 address, the general strategic picture of what has happened is rather easily summed up. It is the question of what happened inside Russia, to accomplish this paradigm-shift in Soviet character and policy, which requires more attention.

If we look at the present situation in terms of reference to the Pugwash Conference, and what we have shown that Conference to imply, we can describe the present situation fairly in the following terms. With Soviet acceptance of the implications of the Pugwash Conference as a "back-channel" for shaping the strategic policies of nations, Moscow implicitly accepted from the start the perspectives of world-government embedded in the design, initiation, and composition of that Conference. The pervading thematic feature of the Conference, from the late 1950s through to the present date, is the division of the entire world into two, or possibly three "empires" of the Persian-Roman empire model, sometimes called "world federalism." Two of the possibly three such empires were foremost, of course, the emergence of one system of world-government in the West, and another in the East, the latter the Russian Empire, or, if one insists, the Soviet Empire. By 1972-1973, it was already clear, even from outside the Conference and related forms of "back-channel" proceedings themselves, that the long-term significance of "détente" was a trend toward a unified system of world-government, based on developing strategic guidelines of regulating conflicts between the two principal empires.

Yet, it was also clear, that the Western spirit of the UNNRA period in Eastern Europe and the 1956 Hungarian and Polish affairs, had not passed from the minds of Western policy-makers. Events in Czechoslovakia in 1968 were a prominent reminder. The West intended to cheat on the "New Yalta" terms of agreement between the two proposed dominant empires. The West intended to "balkanize" the Soviet Empire, and so destroy it from within, by aid of what we term today "integrist" insurgencies. No durable "détente" between the two proposed, principal empires, was possible; one and only one of the two must exert world hegemony.

This associated feature of the "détente process" was not overlooked by the Soviet leadership. The included response of the Soviet leadership was almost instinctive, and not lacking in precedent.

In 1927-1928, following a campaign which almost exterminated the Russian Orthodox Church (among others), the Soviet State Security Organization, then the Cheka, coopted the much-reduced leadership of the Church as Chekist assets. This connection between the Chekists and Church hierarchy appeared to have no more than the obvious kind of implications until 1943. During the preparations for and onset of the Nazi drive to the East, "Operation Barbarossa," the Russian churches had financed the Nazi attack, to a not insignificant degree, and sections of the Soviet population, especially in the Ukraine, had welcomed the Nazis as liberators at first. The defection of General Vlassov's Soviet army was a particularly frightening development for Stalin et al. In 1943, Stalin took a walk into St. Basil's Cathedral in Moscow, engaged for hours with the Russian Orthodox Patriarch. They made an agreement. This was reflected rather immediately, on Stalin's part, by his christening the war the "Great Patriotic War" to save the holy soil and people of "Mother Russia" from the German transgressor. The Church, in turn, mobilized the population in support of the war, and leading Soviet propagandist, Ilya Ehrenberg, writing regularly in *Pravda*, became a fanatical racialist beyond the far limits which Nazi propaganda chief Josef Goebbels imposed upon his department in such matters.

After the War, Stalin maintained the agreement with the Church, to the point of deploying a large effort by combined Chekist and Church forces, in the effort to move

Bertrand Russell's Dream of World Empire

the headquarters of the entire, world-wide Orthodox Church, from Constantinople, to Moscow. President Harry S. Truman, with British help, stopped that in 1952. The abrupt death of Chekist boss Beria, and the Khrushchev period appears to have halted the pace of the growth of the Church's role in the Soviet government; over the 1960s and 1970s, this Church role accelerated, with significant encouragement from agencies in the West. In the West, especially the United States, the view appeared to prevail without question, that since religion is counterposed to "atheistic Communism," the rise of power and influence of religious organizations in the Soviet Empire could accomplish nothing but an eminently desired effect: insurgency against the Soviet state.

The evident Soviet response to the threatened "integrist" insurgencies was consistent with Stalin's actions of 1943-1952, but became much more far-reaching and profound. How much of this was intentional among some Soviet leaders, and how much the inevitable, but unforeseen consequence of a less profound shift intended at the start, is for specialists to determine some future day or other. The fact is, that the collapse of the influence of the Marxist world outlook in the Soviet empire's leading circles, notable already during the middle to late 1960s, created a vacuum, an ideological vacuum filled by something left over from long before October 1917. If it was, at the beginning, merely intended to use religion as a cultural weapon of Soviet state domestic and foreign policies, in fact the weapon adopted largely took over the shaping of the cultural matrix of the Soviet population and leading state institutions, including the Soviet foreign policy institutions and no less than large and powerful elements of the Soviet KGB.

Overall Soviet strategy is presently most clearly visible.

In military policy, as such, the Soviet leadership follows

There Are No Limits to Growth

a policy of practice consistent with the strategy for winning a thermonuclear war first published by Soviet Marshal V. D. Sokolovskii in his first, 1962, edition of *Military Strategy*. The pivotal feature of that strategy is the development of strategic ABM defense systems based on "new physical principles," such as high-powered lasers, as Sokolovskii specified already in 1962, a development in which the Soviet Union is relatively well-advanced today. At the same time, unlike the NATO alliance, the Soviet Union maintains a war-winning capability in massed "conventional" war-fighting forces in depth, land and air forces designed to fight war in the environment of nuclear, bacteriological, and chemical (ABC) weapons deployment. The other notable, added feature, has been the massive concentration on build-up of strategic potentials of the Soviet navy.

The Soviet strategy is relying upon a continued descent of the West into the important condition of "post-industrial societies," with the military correlatives of that decline, to create a condition, perhaps during the 1990s, in which the Soviet Union's deployment of space-based and other elements of a comprehensive strategic ABM defense system capability affords it assured victory of the NATO and allied forces: unchallengeable world hegemony.

The chief military problem of the Soviet leadership is the risk that the West might launch a preemptive thermonuclear attack against the Soviet Union prior to the point that the U.S.S.R. has a deployed strategic ABM defense system. The likelihood of such an assault from the West is determined by the fact that at some moment, a moment when the West has lost the opportunity to match the Soviets in strategic ABM systems development, a moment when the West sees its capabilities for future military defense flickering out of existence, sheer desperation might prompt the West to be willing to risk

Bertrand Russell's Dream of World Empire

thermonuclear war--to prevent continued Soviet build-up-- and not bluff in taking that risk.

Therefore, the leading Soviet concern for the duration of the 1980s (approximately) is to lull the West into the political state of mind of governments and populations, under which state of mind's influence, the West would allow the point of no return to pass with no substantial actions to prevent consolidation of Soviet assured world hegemony during some period of the 1990s.

On this latter count, the nuclear freeze, peace, and Nazi-steered "environmentalist" movements become a principal asset of Soviet strategy. As we readily observe from day to day, the principal instrumentality through which the Soviet KGB organizes these mass movements in Western Europe and the United States is the corrupted leaderships of the Protestant and Catholic churches. There are other features of the operation, but the churches are the primary Soviet KGB channel of influence over mass movements in the West. The principal KGB channel for steering those corrupted church leaderships in the West is the Byzantine Rite's churches, including the coordination of the Byzantine Rite through the extraordinarily influential monasteries situated at Holy Mountain, Greece's Mount Athos. This latter capability, at Mount Athos, the KGB built up massively over the course of the 1970s.

So far in this account of Soviet strategic posture, it would appear to be the case that Moscow is not pushing Malthusianism at home, but only for KGB export to the West. Are they really Malthusians, or is it all part of the psychological warfare theatrics of the KGB?

For the answer to that question, we must look deeply into what is sometimes called the "Russian soul." By seeing the roots of Russian Malthusianism, slightly different than the variety familiar to us from experience and history of modern Western Europe and the United States, the contrast helps us to understand better many things about European history as a whole, including a deeper understanding of the kind of mentality which produces the Western version of Malthusianism.

Religion, Culture and Malthusianism in Russia

The Slavic tribes to the north were among the persisting problems facing Byzantium into and beyond the nominally Christian conversion of Vladimir of Kiev Rus in A.D. 988. Two general approaches were developed during the period prior to Vladimir's conversion. The first approach was predominantly a military one. The second approach, which ultimately prevailed, was the creation of a synthetic form of pseudo-Christianity, which became the foundation for nominal Christianity among the Slavic populations which came under the direction of Byzantium.

The synthetic pseudo-Christianity manufactured for the Slavs was generically a form of *Gnosticism*. From the time of the Emperor Constantine, into approximately the period of the Paleologues, the imperial court sought to impose, top-down, upon the Byzantine Church pseudo-Christian cults based on the pagan cults of the Roman imperial pantheon. The case of Constantine's appointment, Bishop Arius, is typical of the process which continued over centuries thereafter. Religious beliefs recognizably Christian were generally limited to the Greek-speaking population of the East, those seeking to maintain classical Greek literature and language, especially the writings of Plato. The imperial court was forcibly anti-Greek, even to the point of for a time outlawing the teaching of classical Greek and prohibiting a subject of the empire from calling himself Greek or being designated Greek. Despite Christian resistance from among the Greeks, the Church hierarchy at the top was rabidly Gnostic, using Aristotle as the official Church philosopher of pseudo-Christian Gnosticism. This was the real issue between the Eastern and Western Christian churches from the time of St. Jerome and St. Augustine through the 1439 Council of Florence.

The most dangerous of the Gnostics was a faction called the *hesychasts*, originally based by the Emperor Constantine at the St. Catharine's monastery in the Sinai. The rise of Islam prompted shifting the principal center of hesychasm within the empire to what is commonly called today the collection of monasteries on the Holy Mountain, Mount Athos. This hesychastic center, which maintains its traditions to the present day, is presently the world-center of the so-called "integrist" movements, including the various forms of "liberation theologies" and "charismatic" cults created under direction of the Jesuits.

The form of pagan religion which these hesychasts (e.g., navel-contemplators) adopted as a model for constructing a charismatic pseudo-Christianity of the Slavs was the "Mother Goddess" cult already well established in that area--a practice repeated by the Jesuit synthesizers of "tribalist" and similar pseudo-Christian cults today. ("Hey, fellow, so you practice human sacrifice," says the Jesuit, in effect, "you may not know it, but that is consistent with Christianity.")

The "Mother Goddess" is sometimes called *Cybele-Sybil*, the Chaldean *Ishtar*, the Egyptian *Isis*, or the ancient Harrapan *Shakti*. In pagan religions of this grouping, she is associated with a male figure, who is usually a castrated phallus-god, such as *Osiris* or the Harrapan *Siva*, or the Egyptian triad of *Isis, Osiris*, and *Horus*, or in the version used as a model of the pseudo-Christianity of Kiev Rus, the Phrygian *Dionysos* (equal to *Osiris* or the Semitic *Satan*, as *Apollo* is otherwise named *Lucifer*). This pagan model, with hesychastic mystical elements added, was the cultural matrix which Byzantium superimposed upon the existing paganism of Norman-ruled Kiev Rus.

The general model used by Gnostics was followed. In that model, the Holy Family is used to supply new names for Isis (Mary), Osiris (Joseph), and Horus (Jesus). The legends and other myths associated with the pagan belief are then attributed to the members of the Holy Family. In this instance, the mystical "Mother Russia" was employed, together with the pagan belief that the Russian People sprang mystically from the soil which is Mother Russia's body, and that the Will of the People collectively is an expression of the Mother's will: *the Holy Blood and Soil of Mother Russia.*

Although this sort of belief flowed through the Slavic Byzantine churches over approximately a thousand years, the case of the revolt of the so-called Old Believers (*Raskol'niki*) reaching an initial height during the time of Czar Peter I, illustrates the way the cult of Holy Mother Russia permeates the unchurched and even avowedly atheistic populations most efficiently. This revolt of the Old Believers erupted during the late seventeenth century when leaders of the Church proposed to clean up some of the worst corruptions of what passed for the Russian Bible. When Peter I broke with the Third Rome version of the czardom and attempted both to "westernize" Russia and clean up the Church hierarchy from the top, religious eruptions, including mass suicides, among the *Raskol'niki* erupted with a scope and force to make the notorious Rev. Jim Jones appear the dullest of Sunday School teachers. Probably a quarter or more of the Russian population was caught up in this wild and weird cult phenomenon.

During the nineteenth century, the writings of Dostoevsky, especially his *Crime and Punishment,* provide a deep insight into the mental map of the *Raskol'niki* of that century. Another apostle of the *Raskol'niki* tradition, Count Leo Tolstoy, shows most directly what the Raskol'niki version of Malthusianism means. The anarchist assassins of the *Peoples' Will* organization, the nihilists, portray another *Raskol'niki* outbreak, as did the Narodniks into the present century. The Moscow Russian Social-Democratic movement was largely a creature of the *Raskol'niki* who had returned to that city, to become associated with its light industries. The Bolsheviks were saturated with this sort of ideology, as the cases of Bogdanov, Krasin, and Berdyayev illustrate, and also Bukharin. The Bolshevik approach to the problems of agriculture were chiefly shaped by the cult of the commune which flows in Russia directly from the *Raskol'niki* doctrine of Holy Mother Russia's Blood and Soil.

The 1905 Russian Revolution, in which the Venetian Parvus's agent, L. D. Trotsky, performed a notable role, was, overall, a *Raskol'niki* insurrection in form, content, and inspiration, a virtual replica of the Pugachev insurrection of the eighteenth-century *Raskol'niki*. The same cultural matrix was the mass-based force unleashed by the 1917 revolution, and steered by Lenin into the shaping of the initial forms of the Bolshevik Revolution and state.

A glance at the circumstances and content of the original Third Rome prophecy indicate the way in which such a religious prophecy could persist as an influential intellectual force deeply embedded in the Slavic part of the Byzantine culture over a span of approximately five hundred years.

The first manifestations of a Third Rome cult in Russia erupted in the immediate aftermath of the ecumenical 1439 Council of Florence. The ecumenical Patriarch of Paleologue Byzantium travelled to Russia to spread the good news, that Byzantium's adoption of the *Filioque* version of the Nicene Creed had caused the healing of the Great Schism. He was nearly lynched by his Russian fellow priests. The charge was made that he had made a treasonous pact with the corrupted first Rome, and the fact that this had been accepted by the second Rome, Paleologue Byzantium, signified that the second Rome was now as bad as the first.

Overlook the religious-doctrinal formalities for a moment. The crux of the matter was *a violent, racialist xenophobia of Byzantine Russia against the West*. This kind of xenophobia, erupting from the evil mouth of Ilya Ehrenberg during the last war, has its religious basis in the Nazi-like blood and soil doctrines of the cult of Holy Mother Russia's Sacred Blood and Soil. This is the essence of Russian mysticism, the special meaning of the words "Russian Soul," when spoken by a true son of the *Raskol'niki*. It is Russian Romanticism, with the same implications German nineteenth-century Romanticism had in producing the Nazi phenomenon, the deep attachment to the arbitrary, irrational features of the sensual life.

The *Raskol'nik* is a fanatical materialist by dispostion, which is to say that he is a fanatical hedonist, whose God (Goddess) is the spirit of the soil, and whose mysticism, spirituality is ultimately that of Adam Smith's "Invisible Hand," the unknown link between the irrational will of the individual and some unknowable, all-powerful something, which somehow connects the randomness of the acts of individual, irrational wills, into a grand design. Even Josef Stalin could not rule Russia as a political leader, but only as a "little father," as the czars had ruled before him. The embalming of Lenin's body, by Krasin et al., was done with the thought that by these means future science would revive Lenin's body to life.

The eruption of the *Raskol'niki* again is therefore not properly astonishing. Bolshevism had adapted itself, from the beginning, to the reality of the *Raskol'niki* as a mass-based force in the opposition to "westernizing" tendencies of the czars, Witte, and so forth. Lenin et al., had attempted to "judo" the *Raskol'niki*'s influence and ideology to make a Bolshevik version of "westernizing" feasible. The ideology associated with the *Raskol'niki* was never absent. As Marxism-Leninism became weakened as a force, the old cultural matrix, epitomized by the *Raskol'niki*, came to the surface.

From this standpoint, President Franklin Roosevelt's approach to Josef Stalin was perhaps ingenious. By affording the Soviet Union an opening to the West based entirely upon cooperation in providing the Soviet Union access to the benefits of Western technology, under circumstances the Soviet Union most needed such assistance, Roosevelt was acting to break through that Byzantine-Slavic isolation which nourished Slavic xenophobia, and strengthened those currents in Russia which, perhaps in their own fashion and in their-own time, would build something useful out of the "electrification plus soviets" emphasis on "American methods" proposed by V. I. Lenin. Instead of Roosevelt's long-view approach, the West cut off Roosevelt's approach, and played a game of "hard cop plus soft cop," in which Russian isolation from, and hatred of the West was intensified, and in which the game of "empire"--Bertrand Russell's game--was offered to the Soviet leadership as the only apparent alternative to an aversive environment verging upon more or less early thermonuclear warfare.

It was the West, by playing the evil game designed by Bertrand Russell, et al., which played upon the millennial potentialities within Russia's Byzantine cultural matrix, to bring forth the Third Rome potentialities of the *Raskol'niki* currents simmering behind the Bolshevik consciences. The effort was wonderfully successful; the West, influenced by Russell, et al., successfully unleashed the Third Rome potentialities within the Soviet population and leadership.

There Are No Limits to Growth

The Leninist form of Marxist cultural matrix was something with which we could have negotiated successfully, with long-term benefits on every account, because it was anti-Malthusian, "westernizing." Lenin himself, acting through his trusted personal emissary, Chicherin, made the offer at Rapallo. Admittedly, the Friedrich Naumann card was played by Lenin and Chicherin; who cares? The offer should have been accepted on its merits, not rejected on the basis of quibblings concerning its variously direct and indirect authorships. The problem of Western civilization, since the time of Charlemagne--most emphatically--has been to break the power of the Byzantine cultural matrix over Eastern Europe, the Balkans, and so forth. Once the East accepted and assimilated technological progress as a basis for collaboration, to mutual benefit, between East and West, the other desired benefits we might desire from the East would come in due course.

What we have done, in effect, is to orchestrate the environment around the Soviet Union, to the effect of bringing forth a "Frankenstein's monster." In our blind idiocy of supporting a "religion" simply because it was a "religion," without examining what that religion was and had been in the history of mankind to date--the Gnostic form of pseudo-Christianity, and its pagan fore bears--we destroyed a weak and impotent adversary, Marxism, to replace it with a powerful and more deadly adversary, a Russia mobilized around the doctrine of the Third Rome.

They hate us because we are "Western," just as Philotheos of Pskov detailed in his "Third Rome" prophecy. They have used the Gnostic currents of our own Western churches to assist them in destroying us from within, and have entered into an alliance with the Sufi Freemasonic networks and the Nazi international, to make the very "Islamic fundamentalism," presumably deployed against them, into an efficient instrument against us. This "Frankenstein's monster," we created, by posing the question of a new Roman Empire to a nation to whom such a proposal signified their world-rule of a "Third and Final form of the Roman Empire."

Thus, we have come near to the end of Bertrand Russell's grand dream of "international socialism," of Russell's dream for world-empire.

4

The Forests and Cities of Mars

Imagine Mars fifty or sixty years from now, and so imagine yourself seeing a square kilometer thickly planted with young trees, each grown already to approximately a meter in height. Is this "science fiction"? Unless we destroy civilization with thermonuclear warfare, or, alternatively, famines and pandemics caused by neo-Malthusian policies, between A.D. 2030 and 2040, there should be a significant beginning of large-scale colonization .of Mars by mankind.

The U.S.A.'s NASA already possessed knowledge of much of the technology needed to begin manned exploration of Mars before the end of the 1960s. Today, we have either solved, or are within less than ten years of solving, two of the greatest obstacles to Mars colonization.

The first of these two problems is the need for improved sources of energy to power space flight, and also to provide sufficiently abundant energy per capita to sustain an Earth-like artificial environment on that nearby planet, or, much closer, the Moon. So far, interplanetary travel, by manned vehicles to the Moon, or robot satellites to Mars and beyond, has been made with slightly adjusted ballistic trajectories; the interplanetary vehicle is coasting for most of the distance it travels. Let us suppose, instead, that we do something to make the space travelers more comfortable, providing them a net rate of acceleration of the space vehicle which produces the effect of the gravity of Earth; let us suppose that, for the first half of its journey from Earth to Mars, the space vehicle increases its speed by an impulse of 32 feet per second, each second. Or, assume

The Forests and Cities of Mars

that perhaps a compromise is made, that we use only half that acceleration. At approximately the mid-point of the journey, the space vehicle decelerates at the same rate. The time required for the trip could be reduced from months--or longer--presently, to weeks.

If we supply each kilogram of weight of a space vehicle no greater acceleration than that of an automobile moving from a stop to 100 kilometers an hour, and sustain this acceleration second by second, day by day, week by week, the speed of that space vehicle will reach what are called "relativistic velocities." The longer the space journey, the higher the average speed at which the space vehicle covers the distance. The question is, from where do we obtain a constant source of power to provide such accelerations constantly over weeks and longer? The answer, known back during the 1960s, and much closer to realization today, is *controlled thermonuclear fusion*, as we noted this technology in our opening chapter.

This controlled thermonuclear fusion is the source of power we require to maintain many of the features of an Earth-like artificial environment on the Moon, Mars, or elsewhere.

We also require controlled thermonuclear fusion for an additional task: as a source of very high energy-flux densities for excitation and amplification of high-powered lasers and relativistic electromagnetic systems generally. The reason more powerful lasers are usually such large assemblies today, some building-sized, is that the energy sources available have very low energy-flux densities. If we power an x-ray laser, for example, with the energy-flux density of a small fission explosion, we greatly decrease the average size of the laser system required for high-powered systems. Using small fission explosions as power sources is not the most highly recommended procedure to which to expose a human operator; we would use this perhaps, only in robotic devices in space. With controlled thermonuclear fusion, we have available potentially much higher energy-flux densities, and the problems of insulating humans are relatively trivial, compared with the fission cases.

High-powered lasers, and related categories of devices, are almost indispensable for space-colonization. There are three general properties of lasers which supply the needed, great advantage. First, like ordinary electrical house current, the laser beam is monochromatic: the energy transported by the beam is transported by a beam of only one frequency, not several or more mixed together, and the peaks and valleys of the beam's oscillations are all in unison. Since such coherent, monochromatic beams are the best organized form of energy transport available, they are the least wasteful. Therefore, a laser beam may have a thousand times or greater efficiency than other kinds of beams. Second, laser beams do not diffuse as does ordinary electromagnetic radiation, and can be tuned to frequencies such that very little energy is lost doing work on the medium through which the beam travels (such as air), but delivers shock-like work with nearly all the energy transported to whatever target is selected. Third, laser beams have what are commonly termed "self-focusing" characteristics. In a manner related to the tuning of a radio station's broadcast beam, the wavelength of the laser beam is tuned to the resonance among the objects upon which it impinges. Generally speaking, the higher the frequency (the shorter the wavelength), the smaller the area of the target to which the laser beam is resonantly tuned.

Dr. Jonathan Tennenbaum has assembled some data shown in the accompanying illustration (Table 3). This illustration compares the frequency of electromagnetic radiation, from ordinary radio waves, through the visible colors, and beyond the ultra-violet into and beyond the gamma-ray part of the spectrum. The wavelengths

The Forests and Cities of Mars

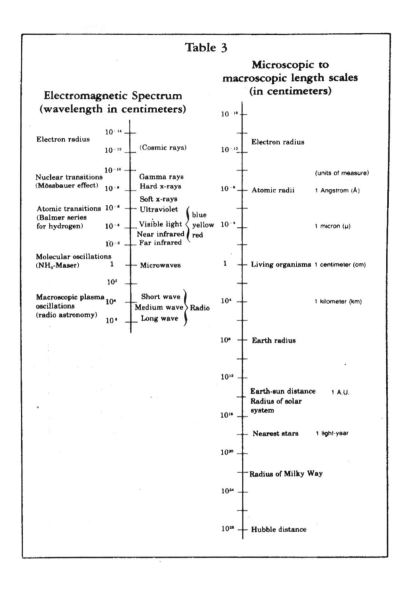

associated with these frequencies are compared, in the adjoining figure of that illustration with the sizes of physical objects, down through small biological cells,

There Are No Limits to Growth

Table 4		
Temperature Increase Through Focusing of Laser Beams		
	1 kW	10,000 kW
Temperatures generated by a laser beam of 1 kW and 10,000 kW per square meter	90°C	3,000°C
Temperature if the beam is focused on 1 mm	11,000°C	110,000°C
Temperature if the beam is focused on the nucleus of an atom	36,000,000°C	360,000,000°C
Temperature if the beam is focused on the radius of an electron (4.6×10^{-15})	8,000,000,000°C	80,000,000,000°C
Comparable Temperatures in Stars: Surface of the sun — 6,000°C; Interior of the sun — 15,000,000°C; Explosion of a supernova — 2,500,000,000°C		

inorganic molecules, down to the scale of the radius of an electron.

Now, look at Table 4. In this table, we have assumed that a laser-like beam transports a quantity of power equal to one kilowatt per square meter. What happens as we concentrate that quantity of power into successively smaller areas? In first approximation what happens can be compared to using a magnifying glass to concentrate sunlight, to the effect of setting fire to paper. We say in the latter case, that we have raised the temperature of the sunlight, by focusing it down to a small area. Therefore, let us ask ourselves what is the rise in temperature which

The Forests and Cities of Mars

occurs as we concentrate the power measured as one kilowatt per square meter into smaller and smaller areas, all the way down to the scale of an electron's radius. Then, for further comparison, repeat the comparison for the case of a beam whose power is equivalent to the energy-flux density of merely a coal-fired industrial energy source, 10,000 kilowatts per square meter, as also shown in Table 3. Finally, compare the temperatures in the areas of highest concentration with known temperatures of the Sun and stars.

This Table presents a very rough, but very useful approximation of the advantages we obtain from high-powered, high-frequency lasers, and from the related categories of devices which are generally called relativistic particle beams. There is no known form of material in the universe which could resist the concentrations of power such beams can transport. On principle, with such technology man could poke holes through the Sun or a star, with effects comparable to cosmic rays. More practical, with such technology's development, we have the power to accomplish controlled transmutation of matter. This technology provides mankind a most useful range of tools.

The two technologies, thermonuclear fusion and laser-like technologies, are very closely interrelated in many describable ways. A properly tuned relativistic beam, properly focused, is an indicated means for producing controlled thermonuclear fusion. The controlled thermonuclear fusion effected, in turn, is the ideal energy source for such beams. One tendency in using such combined technologies will be to subtract the energy required to produce thermonuclear fusion from the total energy obtained from thermonuclear fusion, and to use the net energy obtained in the form of relativistic beams as a basic working tool of production, and so forth and so on. We may think of a new age of technology now opening up for mankind, *an age of fusion beam technology.*

In addition to fusion beam technology itself, the breakthroughs in physics such technology permits us provides the needed conditions for accelerating progress in medical and biological science. The conditions of space travel, and living on distant planets, at different gravities, in artificial Earth-like environments, defines new dimensions for medicine, and for all forms of animal and plant life which accompany mankind in these journeys. As a by-product of this work, we shall accelerate progress in medicine---accelerate the arrival of the time at which modal life expectancies reach perhaps between 120 and 140 years, without likelihood of the kinds of impairments associated with the aging of tissues today.

Even before the space travelers leaving the Earth-orbiting space-port arrive at Mars, the space vehicle in which they travel will incorporate many of the features of the artificial, Earth-like environment they will encounter when reaching their destination. For space journeys of weeks and months, we enter into engineering and logistics problems which cannot be solved by the methods we presently employ in life-support systems and stowed supplies for a trip to the Moon. The air used by the travellers must be manufactured through reprocessing of carbon dioxide, and so forth. Water supplies must also be manufactured on board the space vehicle. Food, too, must be manufactured on board, at least the greatest portion of the bulk of the food consumed.

Table 5 illustrates the point, by listing the weight and the space occupied by the average consumption of oxygen, water, and solid food per adult person per week. Table 6 compares the number of persons lifted into space-orbit now with the weight of the space vehicle per person, and also compares this with the starting weight of the launching system before firing of rockets, needed to accomplish the

The Forests and Cities of Mars

Table 5
Basic Consumption of Oxygen, Water, and Food Per Week For Space Travelers
Oxygen.. 5.6 kg.
Drinking water .... 15.4 kg.
Other water.. 14.0 kg.
Food... 4.5 kg.
Total per person per week... 39.5 kg.

Table 6	
Requirements for an Earth-Moon Trip	
Weight of Mercury space capsule 1 person	1.3 tons
Weight of Apollo moon rocket (including command and landing vessel) 3 persons	45 tons
Starting weight of Saturn V rocket, which launched the Apollo moon rocket	2,740 tons
Necessary fuel to launch 100 kg into earth orbit	ca. 2 tons
Fuel to transport 100 kg from the earth to the moon and back	ca. 6 tons

lifting of the orbiting vehicle and its passengers into Earth-orbit for a trip to the Moon. Finally, the table compares the pounds of fuel required for taking a 100 kilogram load, from Earth-orbit, for a round-trip to Moon-orbit and relanding on Earth, with the added weight of fuel required to put such a system into Earth-orbit, to begin the round-trip. The supplying of a colony on Mars, or a several weeks-long journey to Mars and back, is not like shipping supplies to U.S. troops in the South Pacific, during World War II.

There Are No Limits to Growth

We have indicated that we have imminently available the energy supplies and special kinds of tools of the fusion beam age of technology. With that kind of technology added to what we have available from the work of the 1960s and 1970s, we can solve part of our logistical problems of colonization of, and travel to Mars by building the space vehicles on the Moon. The optimal procedure, in preparing for the preparatory phases of colonizing Mars, is to set up mining and then manufacturing operations on the Moon. There, we build the space vehicles, for example, for the voyages from Earth-orbit to Mars-orbit. The costs of lifting against the gravity of the Moon are vastly less than lifting the same weight into orbit against the gravity of Earth.

Let us assume that we devote the years of 1990-2020 to Moon colonization, building up perhaps to a level of about one million persons living and working on the Moon, and some tens of thousands working, at any given time, in Earth-orbiting and Moon-orbiting manned stations. The initial phase of work on the Moon would emphasize developing and extending the life-support system on the Moon itself, relying to the utmost on materials which can be produced from resources available on the Moon through use of the levels of technology of the fusion beam age. By approximately 2010, it should be feasible to shift emphasis of work on the Moon to production of space vehicles for intra-solar travel.

During the initial phases of work on the Moon, we must have mastered the methods of biotechnology to be used to produce nearly all of the food requirements of the Moon colonists on the Moon. That will serve as the base line from which to effect improvements. During this period, we shall also begin work in growing various kinds of plants, including trees, on the Moon, as well as animals such as mice, chickens, and whatnot.

The Forests and Cities of Mars

Before plunging into deeper space, we shall do thorough research, on the Moon and in Earth-orbiting stations, on the full range of biological possibilities to be considered in colonization of nearby space, including the special range of problems for medical practice in space travel and on distant colonies. Most important, we shall study thoroughly the effects on people of living in space, and the problems of animal life associated with gestation and birth in low-gravity artificial Earth-like environments.

With relatively abundant energy supplies, and vastly improved technologies for using it, one of the most irritating features of nature for scientists and administrators will be the poor performance of biological processes in making use of energy available in larger flux densities. We cannot blame the plant species of Earth for their poor performance on this account; in the opening chapter, we indicated the relatively miserable power--and relatively monstrous inefficiency of solar power. It is the poor quality of solar power to which the Earth's plant life was obliged to adapt itself. Considering the fact that that plant life "invented" chlorophyll, we must congratulate our plant species for doing as well as they have done, in managing to produce our biosphere, despite the miserly treatment our plants have suffered at the hands of the Sun. Now, as we make available to plants much higher energy-flux densities, available to the friendly plants in almost any form they might desire their energy nourishment to be served to them, we must somehow communicate this good news to our plant species. In brief, we must accelerate the reproductive rates of useful biomass, especially as food. Chemists, such as G. Liebig and L. Pasteur, started us on this road during the last century; now in the age of fusion beam technology, we must take a giant step forward along the same road.

The first steps toward colonization of Mars should begin approximately A.D. 2025-2035, or perhaps earlier if

There Are No Limits to Growth

Most of what is necessary for colonization of Mars will be prefabricated on the Moon. The amount of energy consumed in transport from the Moon to Mars is small, because of the Moon's low gravity.

progress of science and economy permits this. With the fusion beam technology, and biophysical technology of the years 2025-2030, the preparations of Mars' colonization will present vastly less difficulty than did the pre-colonization of the Moon thirty or so years earlier. For one thing, Mars already has an atmosphere, a thin atmosphere by Earth standards, but some raw material for our colonizing engineers to begin with. In due course, we shall probably work to build up Mars' atmosphere, but we shall probably begin with artificial environments in bubble-covered agro-industrial complexes, with our agriculture largely hydroponic,.

The colonists from Earth will not be satisfied with that. One can hear a child's voice: "But Daddy where are the trees?" We shall foresee that child's question. We shall have a forest or two on Mars even merely because people like trees, and the idea of having really living, singing birds and so forth, will make the strange planet much more like home. Perhaps it is a bit of a luxury for our colonists in space, but not a wasteful one; trees are very useful for the environment, if properly selected and biologically trained. In any case, our artificial atmosphere will require approximately a standard 47 percent relative humidity, and bubble-covered artificial environments are excellent conditions for producing controlled rainfall.

The Forests and Cities of Mars

Building an agro-industrial complex on Mars will be, by our present Earthly standards, a very costly business. This is no cause for worry. Cost is a relative matter. The true cost of anything, from the standpoint of society, is what percentile of the total labor force available is required to satisfy requirement for product of that specific category of consumption. Fifty years from now, the average power of an adult human being to accomplish work should increase by approximately a factor of ten. In the United States, for example, there should be approximately a threefold leap before the year 2000, chiefly as a result of introduction of laser technology on a broad scale. Although there may be a shift to kinds of materials which are relatively more costly than those generally used today for some categories, a majority of the increased productive power of labor will be a net gain for humanity, such that humanity fifty years from now should be able to afford expenditures eight to ten times as great as today. Among the things Earth should be able to afford fifty to sixty years from now, will be to place up to a million or so human beings into colonization of Mars. Or, perhaps this will occur over the course of a quarter-century; the exact timespan, the exact population need not be foreseen today.

Earth-Mars emigration will be more or less on the scale of operations of nineteenth-century arrivals of immigrants at New York's Ellis Island. The transit will perhaps be approximately within the range of mid-nineteenth-century ocean voyages, and the physical comfort of the travelers perhaps significantly better. The space vehicles assembled chiefly from sub-assemblies built on the Moon for this immigration will be approximately on the scale of ocean liners. This size will be desired for reasons of economy, among other reasons.

The chief item of cost in this migration, from the

standpoint of the Earth's surface economy, will be the cost of delivering a passenger to the Earth-orbiting space passenger terminal" from the surface of the Earth. Otherwise,.the chief item of cost to the economy of the Earth s surface will be getting the capital goods-producing capital goods of fusion beam technology into space, together with the core of bio-technology required. Most of the remainder used will be built on the Moon in orbiting laboratory-factories, or on Mars itself. It will be well-organized pioneering.

The work of the Mars colonists, from the beginning to a fairly advanced point in the progress of emigration, will be maintaining themselves and extending the artificial environment and facilities to accommodate the next wave of arrivals of immigrants from Earth. Ask the colonists why they emigrated, and many would say something equivalent to Sir Edmund Hilary's answer when he was asked why he ascended Mount Everest: "It was there." As for the work they do, the answer would be something to the effect: "We enjoy it." Others would say, that the colonization of Mars is a necessary stepping stone to something much greater; this answer would be closer to the real truth.

The first arrivals on Mars from Earth would be explorers, reminding the oldest among us today of the U.S. Rear Admiral Richard Byrd's voice, back about fifty years ago, broadcasting from the tiny settlement called "Little America," where he stayed throughout an Antarctic winter. The hopes and imaginations of many on Earth would turn to Mars as the first voice and video broadcasts from Mars were received. The first settlements would be dominated by prefabricated components produced for this purpose on the Moon, chiefly. Later, as the exploration expanded, the colony would begin to take the form of a self-sustained expansion of the artificial environment.

The Forests and Cities of Mars

The rate of expansion of the colony by immigration would be a function of the size of the labor force, with the qualification that the rate of growth of per capita rates of expansion through immigration would generally increase as the settlement grew. In other words, the rate at which the colonies on Mars could assimilate new waves of immigrants would grow geometrically, as healthy organisms should.

For the sake of illustration, we shall examine the highlights of the tentative design this writer would project for the Mars settlements on the basis of what is known today.

The settlements on Mars should be built as any sensibly built city or town on Earth should be built today: a layer cake, with the people's habitations and places of work in the top layer, and transportation and basic services distribution in lower layers. The city or town is built from the bottom layer on up, in such a manner that the builders have anticipated needed repairs and more than a century ahead. Perhaps, in some cases, the entire city or town would be built underground, as would probably be the case on the Moon; in general, the same layer cake design for the city would probably persist in most cases.

The basic design of the city or town as a whole would be circular, out of regard for interrelated physical and g topological principles. The center of the city or town would be a tree-festooned park, within which scientific and related educational centers would be located. Along the circular rim of this park area, the principal administrative and cultural functions of the city would be located. The "working-surface of the city" would be the outer rim of the circular area it occupies, with population services distributed along the avenue-like radii extended from the central park to the rim area.

There Are No Limits to Growth

Since the populations in space colonies would usually be living (at least, in all presently foreseeable cases) in an artificial, Earth-like environment, the city must be constructed with an eye to basic principles of safety appropriate to those circumstances. Let us presume that we are referring to a bubble-covered city on Mars. In this case, each city might have a second bubble over, the central park area, which can be closed off from the general environment under the main bubble, if needed. Each dwelling structure and each dwelling unit would be capable of being serviced centrally as a self-contained artificial environment, with a back-up, temporary emergency life-support system within the unit in the case of temporary interruption of access to general services. There would also be emergency areas in the transportation and sub-surface service layers of the city. The city should be as fireproofed as possible, but we must have built-in, convenient, and efficient means for localizing the effects of fires and other possible, temporary contaminations of the artificial environment.

The colonization would take the form of networks of such bubbles, the bubbles linked to one another by two-layer strips, with transportation of people and freight on top, and services below. Some of the bubbles would be cities proper, centers of habitation, science, education, administration, and dwelling, with a peripheral "working-surface" of industries suited to be included within the artificial environment of the city itself. In addition to city bubbles, there would be industrial and agricultural bubbles. Each bubble would be multiply-connected to other bubbles, each bubble like an organ of a living organism.

The central feature of the transportation system would be vehicles moving by means of magnetic suspension systems, such that the vehicles, individually, or in trains, would each be implicitly a self-contained environment.

The Forests and Cities of Mars

Future designers might develop the cities of colonies differently than we have indicated here, but their designs would have prominent points of similarity to what we have outlined here. Human beings will remain human beings, and society will continue to be society: principles of design based on those considerations cannot change very much. The underlying principles of geometrical physics will not change much either, except in the direction of refinements, improvements of our knowledge on that point. The cities of the future in space colonies will be similar to the form in which cities ought to be built on Earth today, even if they are not, presently, built in that way.

So, there will be probably a population of more than tens of millions on Mars alone by the year A.D. 2100. Before that, the human race will have already been busy with a more challenging possibility, the approximately Earth-sized moon, Titan, of the planet Saturn.

On the surface, according to the Voyager reports and their analysis, Titan would be a most unpleasant place in which to live right now. Nonetheless, it has a desirable gravity, a convenient size to match, and the chemical composition of its atmosphere, while presently disastrous to breathe, is a very good raw material for the kinds of transformations we would desire to effect. With abundant energy, at high energy-flux densities, and so forth, by the middle of the coming century, we should be able to begin transforming Titan's atmosphere and surface in the direction we desire. We call this "Earth-forming" a planet. Given the level of fusion beam technology and bio-technology about the middle of the next century, it would appear to be the case from today's standpoint, that the Earth-forming of Titan might be a more attractive proposition for the next century's undertakings than the nearby planet, Venus.

There Are No Limits to Growth

For the project, the Earth-forming of Titan, the probable logistical base of operations will not be Mars, but rather the Earth's friendly, nearby Moon. Mars is nearer to Titan, of course, but the comparative gravities of the Moon and Mars is a decisive economic factor. Besides, by the middle of the next century, the mining and manufacturing on the Moon will be well-developed. Probably, the Earth's astronauts will become, predominantly, recruits from the ranks of the colonies on the Moon and from the orbiting stations around the Moon, Mars, and so forth. Some of this is informed supposition, admittedly, but it is perhaps the best supposition available on the subject today.

There will be jokes, perhaps, which wittily describe the crews of the space-liners as "lunatics," and refer also to the elongation of the physiques of plants, animals, and persons living in low-gravity environments. At least, that would be consistent with any extension of the popular habits of nations today into the middle of the next century.

Rather soon, the Earth should make a leap by about two orders of magnitude in deploying robotic probes into space. Already, we ought to be able to assemble a nuclear-powered, robotic probe system, intended to probe the solar system, among the planets, and the nearby space above the plane of the planets' orbits. Desirable would be a spaceship of sorts, which deploys robotic observation stations into orbits around interesting planets and moons. Our nearby Moon, as well as Earth-orbiting space stations, would be a proper instrument for collecting the broadcast reports from these probes daily, transmitting the collected data to receiving stations on Earth.

With progress in the age of fusion beam technologies, and accompanying advances in bio-technology, the solar system and implicitly the galaxy as well becomes mankind's home base for whatever may occur later on. We can assemble space vehicles which are almost describable

The Forests and Cities of Mars

as planetoids, with aid of factories on the Moon. These space vessels will be each a self-sustaining little society of space explorers, in vessels which can be accelerated to large velocities. The vessels will travel either to fixed destinations, or perhaps along a route defined by fission-powered robotic stations orbiting planets and moons of our solar system, and so forth: and this in delayed, but otherwise efficient regular communication with the main populations of the human race.

On board these exploring space vessels will be the tools of exploration. They will be a space age version of the Ecole Polytechnique under the leadership of the famous Gaspard Monge and Lazar Carnot. These will be bio-astrophysical expeditions, bio-astrophysical laboratories moving in assigned routes in nearby space. Any planet or moon which might be Earth-formed will be given special study by these explorers, studying all matters with a thoroughness not possible with mere robotic probes.

Such space vessels will be populated with scores of scientists, the crew, and the families of scientists and crew. Each will be a university community flying through space, always in continuous direct or relayed communication with the main centers of human civilization. The journeys may be of several, a dozen, or scores of years, perhaps exploratory vessels travelling in pairs or trios of vehicles never more than a few days' distance from one another. This is informed supposition, not firm and fast prediction; supposition or not, we shall do something in the domain of manned exploratory flight to accomplish the same purpose.

Space age pioneering, like pioneering in general, is the occupation of young adults. The colonization of the Moon and Mars will draw off a perceptible portion of the young adults from Earth, especially among young adults with the education and skills needed for such pioneering. From a few hundreds and thousands annually, in the early phases,

There Are No Limits to Growth

to hundreds of thousands annually, then, and more later. The Moon, Mars, exploratory space travel, and such challenges as the Earth-forming of Titan and Venus, will occupy attention increasingly. By the end of the next century, we shall be thinking in terms of the foreseeable time that the human population living somewhere else than on Earth is the largest part of the human population.

Why shall we do this? What is the purpose behind such developments of the century ahead? For the reason Sir Edmund Hilary gave for ascending Mount Everest--"Because it is there"? For sake of curiosity, love of adventures? Perhaps, because of a desire to spread life among the barren planets and moons, to the extent we are able, to feel thus less alone in the universe around our planet? Out of love for life? Certainly not to deal with "overcrowding" on Earth, although perhaps, in many cases, to enjoy the challenge of mastering an area less crowded.

The most profound thinkers among scientists will direct this space effort to *a religious purpose*, a purpose consistent with St. Augustine's emphasis upon insertion of the *Filioque* into the Nicene Creed.

Mankind is unique. The same creative powers of mind which enable mankind to increase willfully the potential relative population density of our species on Earth by three orders of magnitude, are a creative power to discover, ever more perfectly, that lawful composition of the universe by which the universe as a whole is governed. For the religious thinker who accepts the principle of the *Filioque*, those higher principles of lawful composition of the universe are reflections of the *Logos*, which some translate as "Holy Spirit." This Logos is not some wisdom to be contemplated in the manner of a monk in a monastic retreat; it is knowledge which must guide our actions, our labor. To whatever labor this knowledge leads us, we must act accordingly.

The Forests and Cities of Mars

It is not necessary for mankind to know in advance what duties of labor that Logos's guidance shall require of us in space. We shall go into space exploration for the minimal purpose of discovering what we cannot discover merely sitting on the surface of this planet. The mere fact that we know that there are defects in our knowledge of the lawful composition of the universe is sufficient *practical* reason for space exploration. We already know, from the achievements of NASA, for example, that everything we develop in the course of preparing the exploration of space has rather immediate benefits in terms of the conditions of life on Earth; that *practical* benefit will be sufficient motive for some. For others among us, we shall be driven by the need to discover what duties await mankind as a result of the knowledge and increased capabilities developed in that effort.

Astronomy has a very special place in the history of human culture. Since the time of Johannes Kepler, and later, during the lifetime of Karl Gauss, we have known that some of the poetic epics transmitted by oral tradition into such written forms as the Vedas have contained highly accurate calculations of long astronomical cycles, including one longer than 200,000 years. It was Kepler's solar hypothesis, an improved version of a solar hypothesis posed approximately a hundred-fifty years earlier by Cardinal Nicholas of Cusa, an hypothesis already found within the "Paradise" canticle of Dante Alighieri's *Commedia*, which established the foundations of modern mathematical physics as a comprehensive body of knowledge. When we wish to speak of underlying truth, we speak of higher truths, and point upwards--to the stars.

Whence in ourselves comes this reaching toward the stars?

Individual mortal life is notoriously brief. If a person devotes his or her life to matters of personally experienced pleasure and pain, as David Hume, Adam Smith, Jeremy Bentham, and John Stuart Mill insist, then what comes out of such a life excepting memories of pleasure and pain, memories which are buried with our dead bodies? Such a man lives, morally, like a beast, and dies like a beast. There is no purpose to his life, such that his living is directed to some valid purpose, a purpose which is of benefit to the generations which come after him.

What is the nature of those benefits which might live after us? Are they things built? What we build well may serve mankind after us, and contribute to some higher purpose in that way. Yet, things built are consumed, or consumed by time. What, then, endures, after they have been consumed? If this which endures is not "things," what is it?

What endures is our contribution to the advancement of culture. By advancement of culture, we must signify an increase in the creative powers of mind of those who come after us. We measure "advancement" in terms of the power of minds to effect increases in the potential relative population density. It is not the material benefits of such advances which is fundamental to us morally, although those material benefits may be necessary to fostering the moral advancement. The importance of consistent advances in potential relative population density, is that the consistency of such advances in potential proves that the direction which creative discovery and policy-decision gives to changes in human practice are consistent with the lawful composition of the universe. This signifies proof that the direction supplied by a certain method of successive advances in creative discoveries is consistent with the lawful composition of the universe, is in that degree in agreement with the Logos. It is the transmission of an improvement in such directedness of the creative-mental process which is provably an advancement of

The Forests and Cities of Mars

culture.

Even though that which we contribute will we hope be surpassed by those who come after us in the process of being surpassed it enters into the necessary foundations of that which supercedes it. Whoever contributes to such foundations has lived a necessary life.

What then, is true pleasure? Is true pleasure not the Joy of knowing that one is acting in such a manner that one's life will have been necessary to humanity after one is dead? Is true pleasure not a consciousness of that quality? Is true pleasure not the power to be conscious of those moments of one's activity in which that quality is served?

This pleasure can assume many forms, in respect to particular kinds of activity. A child or youth, assimilating the development of his or her potentials, has available the pleasure of a process of rediscovery which is an original experience for the child or youth. This pleasure is delight in the development of powers to accomplish good. In addition, the child and youth are learning which principles of discovery are reliable guides to creative judgment--if the educational process is based on such principles. The student is learning the joys of Reason. The workman whose factory labor may be repetitive at the moment, may, nonetheless, be making possible a creative endeavor, and has, therefore, the right to participate in the sense of pleasure of the creative endeavor served. A parent who nurtures a child into creative potentials, deserves great pleasure from anticipating the benefits to mankind this implies.

Whatever contributes to such a process of advancement of mankind's culture is good. A higher good is that which influences the institutions of society, to the effect society better promotes and nurtures such individual good among all members of society, and nullifies that which prevents good. Such improvements in society preserve a thousand goods of the sort one individual may otherwise contribute.

Before leaving this immediate topic, we are obliged to restate the same point in a rigorous way. No principle can be identified as being as important to all mankind as we have implied this principle to be, without being stated in a rigorous fashion. What exactly do we signify by the principle of creative discovery to which we have referred in the immediately preceding paragraphs?

All discoveries which have the form of rigorously scientific discoveries occur in one among three possible forms. Each form of discovery occurs as empirical demonstration of an *hypothesis*. There are three distinct levels of hypothesis:

1. *Simple Hypothesis*. In forming a simple hypothesis, one assumes that existing scientific knowledge in general is correct as far as it goes, and that the knowledge pertaining to some one or more particular aspects of scientific work in general is, similarly, correct as far as it goes. One assumes, additionally, that the valid explanation of some additional matter must be not in *principled contradiction* to the existing knowledge of related matters. One formulates an hypothesis which may be broadly described as *rigorously consistent with existing scientific knowledge*.

2. *Higher Hypothesis*. This is the sort of hypothesis associated with scientific revolutions. In this case, opposite to the case of simple hypothesis, one assumes that prevailing scientific knowledge includes some identified fundamental error of underlying assumption. One selects some experimental test adequate to prove that that indicated assumption is indeed in error, and some different assumption correct.

3. *Hypothesis of the Higher Hypothesis*. In this case, we begin with the assumption that the successive scientific

The Forests and Cities of Mars

revolutions associated with provable advances in knowledge can be studied for the purpose of discovering some common principles of discovery. We are seeking *a principle of discovery*, which, applied to existing levels of scientific knowledge's advancement, will *predictably* produce a higher hypothesis leading to a successful scientific revolution.

To the best of our present knowledge, these distinctions were first presented by Plato, who included the hypothesis of the higher hypothesis as a methodological principle used in his *Timaeus*. In the *Timaeus*, Plato causes Socrates to name God "the Composer," and to propose to the participants in this dialogue that they review what is known of the principles of composition by which the universe is ordered in the manner presented to our senses. Using the method of the hypothesis of higher hypothesis to treat a fundamental and universal principle of geometry, Plato, at the end of the dialogue, equates the principle underlying the hypothesis of the higher hypothesis with the Logos, and states that this Logos is the efficient will of the Composer, and is of the same substance as the being of the Composer. This is known in Christian theology as the principle of *consubstantiality*.

In the Gospel of St. John, for example, the equation of God to the Logos, as *consubstantial*, is the beginning. St. Augustine later emphasizes that this signifies that the Logos flows through Christ and from Christ as from God. The entire accomplishment of Western civilization, insofar as Western civilization is properly defined as having contributed accomplishments, was the result of the influence of St. Augustine's emphasis on that point, the *Filioque* doctrine.

The connection of theology to practice, on this point, is that if man dedicates himself to the "imitation of Christ" on this essential point, then man must develop and apply his potentialities to the purpose of causing the directing power of the Logos to flow through him into practice. This is *the conception of man, and of man within the universe*, which has determined the best which Western civilization has produced. It is from this vantage point, that we view individual human life as sacred, and place emphasis on the development of the potentialities of each and every member of society, and also upon affording the individual opportunity to effect some fruitful realization of those developed potentialities.

We are not proselytizing for any particular religious confession here. Here, we are merely showing how this view of man, and of man in the universe, occurs within Christianity--at least, in any form of belief for practice which is recognizably Christian. More broadly, this signifies, first, a recognition that life is superior to non-life, and, second, that human life has a divine distinction which distinguishes it as absolutely higher than all other forms of life. Finally, this recognition of the divine quality of the human creative powers of mind, is associated with the will to discover and to be governed efficiently by the Logos.

Except as we adopt and share that view of man, and of man acting practically in the universe, we are morally as beasts, and, it has been shown that when we accept the moral indifferentism to higher principles demanded by David Hume, or in Adam Smith's 1759 *Theory of Moral Sentiments*, we behave as beasts toward one another.

To satisfy the principle reflected in the notion of an hypothesis of the higher hypothesis, we must be engaged continuously in developing successful higher hypotheses, the equivalent of successive, scientific-revolutionary advances in human knowledge. So, working to that end, each of us contributes something of enduring worth to culture. This activity is our pleasure, our source of greatest joys.

The Forests and Cities of Mars

This quality of joy is not a dry, academic sort of miserly gloating over the possessions of knowledge. This joy is associated with the act of giving to humanity, of nurturing the divine potentialities within others, throughout the span of generations yet to come. This is a joyful act of lovingness toward humanity. *Without such love, knowledge is a dead thing.*

That is the joy of loving extended toward each child born. It extends to the whole of human life.

Someone whispers: "The doctors say he is hopelessly ill, and in such pain, too."

Another comments on this: "Why are they letting him suffer, just trying to keep him alive a few more weeks?"

These fools! Who would play God with human life? What do they know of what that dying man or woman may accomplish during the last remaining days of struggling with life? Even an expression of love by, or toward that man or woman, to or from a member of the family or a friend, may be important for humanity in some way.

"But, he is suffering so much, and not conscious."

He is fighting a sickness. He is fighting for the cause of life, and so contributing determination to conquer that illness for all humanity to come, and by his fight adding to the knowledge which may save many others. He is the best of all soldiers, turning even his last days of suffering into something of enduring value for all humanity!

"Perhaps what you say is true, but who will ever remember his small part? Is his tiny contribution worth the suffering he endures?"

Few of us are ever anything but very small in the span of humanity. Shall we, for that reason, kill most of humanity at birth? Is the infinitesimal good their lives will give worth the suffering they will probably endure? Most of the good transmitted by humanity has been the addition of indiscernibly small good done by long-forgotten names. This man's final act of good is perhaps as good as the entire lifetime of many people. Who are you or to judge differently? When did you make yourself God?

Let us pose the question differently. Where lies that man's true suffering? Is it in his pain and other discomforts, or the indignities of his treatment? Or, is the awful thing the fact that without the advantage of hedonistic pleasures, he feels himself useless, a mere burden to society and his family? Is it the fact that he believes that he has little for which to continue to live in such a condition? Is it not that his mere ability to think, and to communicate what he thinks under such circumstances, no longer appears to be of much importance? Is it not that his helplessness confronts him with the fact that he has never really placed much importance on his mind? Is it not that by being reduced to this condition, and judging his mind a worthless value in that condition, he implicitly judges his entire life to have been of no importance at its end? Therein lies his true suffering; he never obliged himself to discover what it was really to live, and being instructed to live by the standards of pleasure and pain, when pain is great, life no longer has value for him. Why, then, do we permit an arrangement of mankind's affairs which leads to such a condition?

Let us each die joyfully with a smiling thought: "It has been a good life, and I will not give up such a beautiful thing while I have the means to stay alive a minute longer." Sometimes it is necessary to hazard death, but only that others and the good may live after us. We may surrender our own lives willfully only for the cause of life, and for the good which life must accomplish. For that reason, we shall grow a forest on Mars.

A study carried out by the Fusion Energy Foundation has demonstrated that a world populated by 10 billion people is absolutely necessary—essential to develop the division of labor required to sustain an economy based on thermonuclear fusion power, the energy source that will enable mankind to undertake space colonization, and wipe out hunger, disease, and misery on earth.

Three of the 19th-century founders of 20th-century fascism: Fyodor Dostoevsky (top left), Friedrich Nietzsche (top right) and Leo Tolstoy.

V. I. Lenin speaking to workers during the Russian Revolution. Lenin's policy was "Socialism is electrification plus Soviet strength."

View of Phobos, a moon of Mars, from the surface of Mars. This view would be seen by astronauts who would use Phobos as an intermediate station for undertakings on Mars.

From left to right: Leonardo da Vinci, Luca Pacioli, Karl Friedrich Gauss, George Cantor, Jacob Steiner, Bernhard Riemann

Clockwise from top: Immanuel Kant, Ludwig van Beethoven, Friedrich Schiller

Above, *St. Augustine in his Study*, by Vittore Carpaccio; below, *Dante* by Domenico di Francesco

The Transfiguration of Christ of the Renaissance painter Raphael (1482-1520). The three levels of human knowledge are represented here. The boy crying out in the lower right of the painting embodies the sensuous level, the apostles in the center that of simple consciousness, and Jesus Christ the divine in man, creativity.

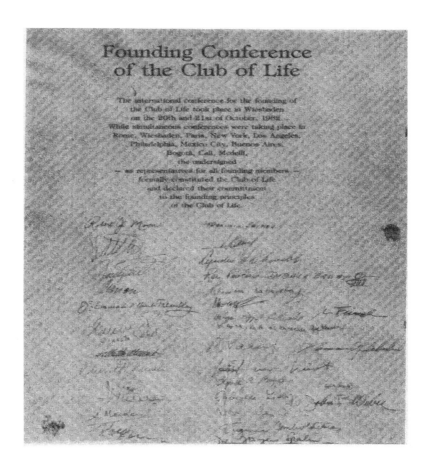

5

The General Law Of Population

In their own fashion, some Malthusian fanatics might be described as "sincere." Can you imagine the following conversation with a "sincere" Malthusian?

Imagine yourself asking a sincere Malthusian: "Can you give me a concrete demonstration that there are too many people?"

To which he replies: "Of course. Take the case of that lazy, good-for-nothing uncle of mine. . . ."

Is this example an exaggeration? Compare this example with the real-life example of one among the proud founders of the Malthusian Club of Rome, former Director of the OECD, Dr. Alexander King. Dr. King volunteered that his motive had been to rid the world of what he considered an excessive number of darker-skinned races. Bertrand Russell, like King, revealed his racialist motives in books he wrote and caused to be published himself. Russell, like King was spiritually a follower of the racialism of Cecil Rhodes and Charles Dilke.

Dilke had written in *Greater Britain*:

> In America we have seen the struggle of the dear races against the cheap--the endeavors of the English to hold their own against the Irish and Chinese. In New Zealand . . . in Australia . . . in India. . . . Everywhere, we have found that the difficulties which impede the progress to universal dominion of the English people lie in the conflict with the cheaper races . . . the dearer are on the whole

144

The General Law of Population

likely to destroy the cheaper peoples. . . . Saxondom will rise triumphant from the doubtful struggle.

This is Russell's passage quoted elsewhere here, from his 1921 *Problems of China*:

. . . the less prolific races will have to defend themselves against the more prolific by methods which are disgusting even if they are necessary.

That is Alexander King's view, the view of the circles, including the Harriman family, around New York City's American Museum of Natural History, praising Hitler's "racial hygiene" policies during a 1932 conference, and the Draper Fund/Population Crisis Committee presently. It is purely and simply Dilke's version of "social Darwinism." The motive is the practice for which we hung Nazis at Nuremberg.

Those are the motives of the "sincere Malthusians," according to their own repeatedly stated account of the matter. That is what the authors of the Club of Rome describe as its true purpose. However, these fellows would not have recruited a mass following among professed liberals if they had splashed their "sincerity" in the matter over the front pages of the mass circulation news media. The propaganda was more diplomatic; in short, they lied, as the case of the hoax, the Club of Rome's *Limits to Growth*, illustrates the point.

Take, for example, the case of the banning of DDT.

The campaign to ban DDT, and other essential pesticides and so forth, began with the publication of the late Rachel Carson's book, *Silent Spring*. According to a decision by the U.S. government later, it has been "proven" that DDT was killing off bird species and doing other terrible things. It was also argued, that DDT did not decompose to any appreciable degree, but continued to poison nature perhaps for centuries, concentrating itself more and more in plant and animal species--the picture painted with complicity of members of the U.S. government was a frightful one. It was all one big lie. The scientific reports used by the government officials who made such frightening statements proved directly the opposite of everything those officials said. Those officials were simply lying.

The development and use of DDT had enabled society virtually to eradicate entire categories of epidemic disease, and had saved so large a percentile of crops throughout most of the world that food supplies had risen as a result of this saving of average per-hectare yields. Since the banning of DDT, agriculture has been forced to rely on pesticides which are in some instances quite dangerous to farm-labor populations, if not handled with more or less precise procedures required for this. For lack of a safe, widely-used substance, DDT, the old epidemics we had defeated earlier have risen and at an accelerating rate since the early-1970s banning of DDT. Crop losses have risen, and disease-related death rates of populations have risen, especially among what Bertrand Russell abhorred as "the more prolific races."

In other words, the fanatical Malthusians of the U.S.A.'s Environmental Protection Agency, itself an outgrowth of the Great Society" paradigm-shift of the middle 1960s, had resorted to one of those "methods which are disgusting even when they are necessary," which Russell proposed.

The standard sort of lying propaganda in support of Malthusianism, since Malthus's popularized plagiarism of Gianmaria Ortes's attack on Dr. Benjamin Franklin, has been essentially the repeated insistence that human

The General Law of Population

populations tend to increase geometrically, whereas, it is alleged, the mineral natural resources of the world are finite, and the animal and plant species grown for supply of human wants increase only arithmetically. This is the sort of lie university professors prefer to tell; if they are caught lying outright by their use of such statements, they can defend themselves with the observation that their actions were not ordinary non-professional lying, but the academically distinguished practice of "scientific lying."

We have already indicated the most general, empirical proof that this professorial sort of argument for Malthusian dogma is factually absurd. The human population has increased by more than two orders of magnitude, and is provably at the brink of reaching a population potential three orders of magnitude--1,000 times--greater than primitive "hunting and gathering society." This could not have occurred if the supply of mineral, animal, and plant resources had not kept pace with the "geometrical" expansion of the human population.

Malthus's false argument on this point was not original to him or Gianmaria Ortes. The argument was originally popularized in Western Europe during the early eighteenth century, by the Jesuits, when it was introduced as the axiomatic assumption in support of the dogmas of the French Physiocrats. According to the researches of this writer's associates, the first influential Jesuit writing to this purpose was the *Description of the Chinese Empire* by the Rev. Duhalde, S.J., which appears to have been based on the same sources from which the founder of the French Physiocratic school, the famous Dr. Quesnay, wrote his *Despotism In China*.

For nearly two millennia, the mandarin system had kept the population of China oscillating, between periods of famine and so forth, at maximum levels of approximately sixty millions, less than the present-day a population of

There Are No Limits to Growth

Thailand, and about half the present level of population of Japan. This was not a trait inherent to the Chinese people. We know that a relatively advanced population and culture had existed in China much earlier than the rise of the Han dynasty, and we know of recurring efforts, even after the mass killing of scholars and burning of books, to develop an advancement in the culture of China with aid of such enterprises as visits to India into the aftermath of the Gupta period. However, the mandarin spy system, under whose terms individuals were responsible to report promptly to authorities the arrival of any "stranger" to a village, served to keep China locked into a system of despotic rule, under which agriculture was kept within rather well-defined, "traditional," labor-intensive methods.

Mainland China today is estimated to have a population in the order of about one billion persons. With large-scale infrastructural projects, some of which have been known to be feasible and desirable for as long as nearly 2,000 years, and modern nuclear, directed beam and biological technology, China could sustain clearly a population well in excess of two billion persons. Naturally, China would require significant cooperation to accomplish all of this, but the projects are technically quite realizable. China's chief predicament on this account, putting aside outside factors, was recently stated to the writer's associates by one official there: "China walks on two legs," one Chinese tradition, and the other the need to employ "Western" technology. How to balance between preserving its rural and related traditions, while using "Western" technology to assist in increasing the productive powers of labor, is the great policy question of China's leaders.

The Jesuits' role in the Subcontinent and Far East during the sixteenth and seventeenth centuries was not a pretty one, not one calculated to enhance the reputation of the Christianity those Jesuits professed to represent, nor make

The General Law of Population

the Westerners especially likable among the peoples of those regions. The Jesuits worked their way into very influential positions in the imperial court of China, and are persuasively documented as having had a hand in overthrowing one dynasty in China. They also insinuated themselves, with disastrous consequences, into the court of the Mogul emperor in India. As for their religious practices, some of these pagan experiments were so flagrant, so embarrassing, that the matter had to be put before the Inquisition.

The Jesuits should not be accused of bringing the drug traffic to the Indian Ocean region, Southeast Asia, and China; that traffic was organized by Arab traders. However, the Jesuits are responsible for fostering its continuation, and the Dutch East India Company for greatly increasing it to the levels at which the British East India Company took over during Adam Smith's time. Such was the enlightenment which the Jesuit missionaries brought back into Western Europe from the Far East, notably including the networks associated with Voltaire, Montesquieu, Diderot, Rousseau, and so forth, as well as the Physiocrats. After all, the Jesuits are a "rib".taken from the Priory of St. John, to form the secret intelligence service of the feudalist Venetian rentier-financier *fondi*; it is that essential fact to which all inquiries into the order and its predominantly political practices must each time return.

The Physiocrat's argument was that the entire wealth of society was derived from the land, and that the amount of wealth which might be extracted was fixed in limit, as the fixed, upper limit of "the bounty of nature." This arbitrary, axiomatic assertion, was accompanied by a second argument, a Jesuit's argument set forth by Adam Smith's superior, David Hume, and restated in Calvinist form by Smith himself. The argument is Smith's insistence, that man must limit himself to the hedonistic pursuit of individual pleasure, and not concern himself with "those beneficent ends which the great Director of nature intended" to accomplish by means of human capabilities. Hume, Smith, Bentham, and the rest of the lot justified the African slave-trade, the China opium-trade, and ruinous usury, on the grounds that man must obey his hedonistic, pleasure-seeking instincts, without regard for any higher moral or natural principles in the composition of the universe. Although the Jesuits professed to be religious, for them religion was merely an arbitrary principle, a principle inaccessible to proof.

The case of René Descartes is exemplary of the Jesuits' view on this point. Descartes's clockwork universe, of points flying about in empty space is, for mathematical physics, what Hume, Smith, and Bentham are for morality. Descartes's mathematical physics permits God to exist only as both the Creator of a clockwork universe, who is no longer permitted to meddle with the universe's affairs since Creation, and as, otherwise, the Being at the other end of the Jesuits' unverifiable, but alleged telephone conversation. God, for Descartes, is not efficiently manifest in nature, and thus only a figment of the imagination, with the Jesuits' fertile and cheerfully inconsistent, and frankly opportunistic imaginations, recommended as the model. God, for the Jesuits, is the mysterious principle embedded in the individual's hedonistic "instincts," as Smith's "Invisible Hand."

This Jesuitical method, this empiricist method, forbids the effort to adduce consistent higher principles from natural processes, and prohibits the attempt to apply the lessons of such scientific inquiry to the shaping of individual policy and actions. All evidence, no matter how massive, contrary to permitted sorts of arbitrary assumptions, such as Physiocratic assumptions, is ruled out of order, simply on the premise that the evidence pertains to

The General Law of Population

examination of some empirically demonstrable universal, higher principle. Such facts as the proof, that humanity has willfully increased its population potential by more than two orders of magnitude, is outlawed.

If a Calvinist kills a man, it is not the Calvinist who has caused this death; the action, according to Adam Smith's 1759 argument, was prompted by the instinctive mechanisms which the Creator built into the Calvinist perpetrator, and the death which occurred is some mysterious consequence of the Creator's Will in embedding such instinctive propensities within the Calvinist. That we must check, alter, what appear to be our instincts on this account, Smith expressly prohibits.

Can we be accused of exaggerating on this point? Are we to be accused merely of drawing the implications of Smith's argument against morality to their logical limit? Can our argument be refuted: Calvinists would not actually carry Smith's argument to such a limit?

Look at the "environmentalist" movements of today. It is provably the case, that the imposition of "appropriate technologies" upon the nations of Russell's "more prolific races," as proposed by the Brandt ("North-South") Commission, must cause a collapse of the potential relative population density of those nations well below the existing levels of population. This is readily shown. We need but consider the rates of depletion of soil subjected to labor-intensive modes of "appropriate technology" in agriculture, and examine the per capita output of labor-intensive modes of other production. This sort of fact is well known to the leading specialists associated with the World Bank, the agency behind the Brandt Commission, and other leading strata of the responsible parties involved. To impose such a policy upon nations is outright mass murder; there is no other word for it.

There Are No Limits to Growth

Nor, can the proponents of "appropriate technologies," at least not the leading proponents with access to scientific information, argue that they do not know that the *Limits to Growth* argument is all a big lie. They are imposing what amounts to mass murder on "the more prolific races" for no other reason than that it pleases them to do so. They are viciously fanatical in their actions against those who consistently object to the immorality of their pleasure-seeking on this point.

They are wont to commit mass murder against hundreds of millions of human beings, chiefly by economic methods, merely to gratify their pleasure.

It is the same with the mass of the "environmentalists." They tell the wildest lies, and ultimately insist that their argument is that they find "industrial society and a regime of "technological progress" psychologically oppressive. To gratify their irrational desires, they demand that the affairs of the world be reordered even if this means mass murder of billions by economic means.

What is the scientific truth which these Jesuits, Physiocrats, Calvinists, and modern Malthusians refuse to permit be brought into consideration? It is to this positive side of the matter that we now turn our attention for the remainder of this book.

What Does "Geometric Increase" Signify?

Two things are most directly proven by the simple fact, that mankind's population potential has been willfully increased by more than two orders of magnitude. This confirms one part of the Malthusian's argument, that human population growth tends to be "geometrical." Simultaneously, the fact that this growth has occurred disproves conclusively that the means to satisfy human wants grow only "arithmetically." Obviously, the growth

The General Law of Population

of the human population since 1798 proves that man can cause the means to satisfy increasing levels of per capita wants to grow more rapidly than the geometrically-increasing population.

The evidence proves that we must focus the entirety of any study of a Law of Population on the matter of "geometrical growth-rates." Since the growth of the human population has been achieved through man's willful alterations of his practice, we must define geometrical growth of populations in terms of some specific kind of willful capacity of mankind.

The first appearance of the idea of geometrical growth-rates, as a mathematical statement, occurred during the twelfth century A.D., as an arithmetic calculation known as *the Fibonacci series*. This arithmetic calculation was constructed in the attempt to measure the increase of animal populations, such as rabbits, without taking into account death-rates. If we subtract the number of deaths occurring simultaneously with births, in each generation, from the number of total births, the Fibonacci series is a good first approximation (Figure.1).

During the last decades of the fifteenth century, in Milan, Leonardo da Vinci and his collaborator' Luca Pacioli proved that the Fibonacci series was a geometrical, not arithmetic series. As the growth of populations becomes very large, the ratio of total populations to populations in successive periods becomes an increasingly close approximation to a geometrical ratio called the Golden Section. Through extensive observations by themselves and their collaborators, da Vinci and Pacioli demonstrated that the growth-rates and morphological features of functions of living organisms--plants, animals, and humans--were all consistent with the same Golden Section.

There Are No Limits to Growth

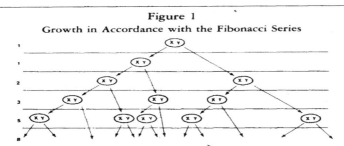

Figure 1
Growth in Accordance with the Fibonacci Series

Growth of an animal population in accordance with the Fibonacci Series: In this simple case, the assumption is made that every pair (xy) lives for two generations and produces one pair of young during each generation. Each of these pairs lives for two generations and dies after producing the second pair of young. If, additionally, each pair of young consists of a male and female animal, which again produce two generations of young, then the growth of this animal population corresponds to the Fibonacci Series.

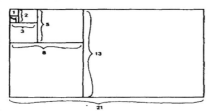

Fibonacci Rectangle: The proportions (long side to the short side) of the ordered rectangles approach the proportion of the Golden Section.

Generation	New born young	Dead pairs	Total number of pairs
1	(1)	0	1
2	1	0	2
3	2	1	3
4	3	1	5
5	5	2	8
6	8	3	13

There is nothing magical, "numerological," in this connection. The Golden Section arises in elementary geometrical constructions in two ways. Both of these constructions are shown to have the same origin, the same basis. An intelligent school child of about twelve or thirteen years of age can master these constructions, and can so understand and prove the principle involved.

The General Law of Population

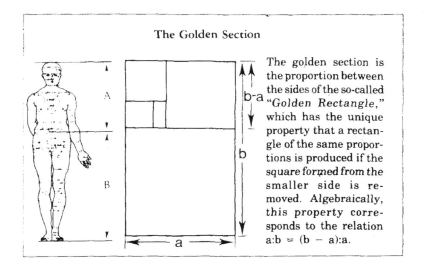

The Golden Section

The golden section is the proportion between the sides of the so-called "*Golden Rectangle,*" which has the unique property that a rectangle of the same proportions is produced if the square formed from the smaller side is removed. Algebraically, this property corresponds to the relation a:b = (b − a):a.

Figure 2
Construction of a Pentagon from a Circle.

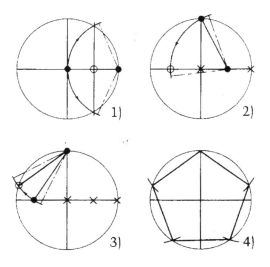

There Are No Limits to Growth

The Golden Section is usually associated with the construction of a regular pentagon, inscribed within a circle. We depict that construction in two ways in Figure 2, once by simple construction from the circle itself, and a second time in terms of construction by means of triangles: Figure 3. There is a second way in which to generate the Golden Section. It is the second way which guides our attention to the deeper meaning of the words, "geometrical growth-rates."

We construct a cone from a circle. For example, we construct a sector of a circle, and by one act of topological folding, produce the differential-topology integral of the sector, a cone. On the cone, starting from the base, we draw on the exterior a line which is always at a constant pitch (Figure 4). Observe the line running down the side of the cone, from the tip (apex) of the cone, to the circular base's perimeter. This line is a radius of the circle from which we constructed the cone. This radius line along the exterior surface of the cone intersects the arms of the spiral drawn around that surface. Now, compare the lengths of the radius cut off by the arms of this spiral. These lengths are such that line segment a is in the same ratio to line segment b, as b to c. This is called a *self-similar* relationship, which is represented in various ways, all equivalent to one another. This spiral is otherwise called a *logarithmic spiral*.

The General Law of Population

Figure 3
Construction of a Pentagon from a Triangle

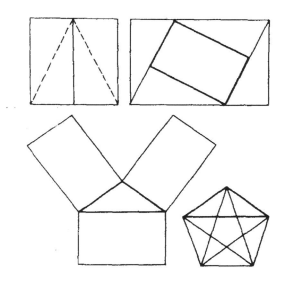

Now, imagine that the material from which we have constructed the cone is transparent. Let us look at the cone from the bottom. What is the figure we see, looking at the spiral on the cone's surface from the bottom of the cone, rather than viewing it from the side? The projection of the 3-dimensional spiral onto the 2-dimensional circular base of the cone is an Archimedean spiral. Now consider the radius line we drew from the tip of the cone to the base (Figure 4). The line segment lengths of that radius line are not in proportions corresponding to the Golden Section.

Now, let us construct the same cone in a different way. Let us imagine that we have a line, the central axis of the cone (Figure 5). Pick a point on this line. Now, imagine, that for each movement away from that point, along the line, there is an action of rotation, such that the radius of

There Are No Limits to Growth

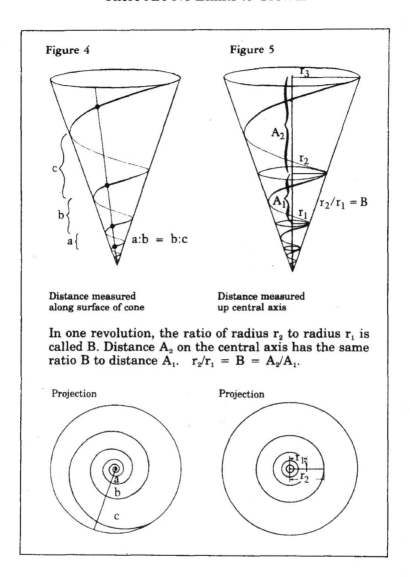

In one revolution, the ratio of radius r_2 to radius r_1 is called B. Distance A_2 on the central axis has the same ratio B to distance A_1. $r_2/r_1 = B = A_2/A_1$.

rotation grows at some continuous rate. For each distance, A, moved along the line continuously in a constant direction, the radius of rotation grows by ratio B, and one complete circular rotation is completed. The result will be a self-similar spiral lying on the surface of a cone. Think of the cone as growing continuously, and think of the amount by which the cone has grown with each complete circular rotation of the spiral. Therefore, after each complete rotation of the spiral, we have the circular base of the growing cone defined. Those successive, circular bases will also be in self-similar proportion, for obvious reasons.

With that step, we have completed the foundations of the *theory of functions of a complex variable*. The conical function which generates such a cone is the most primitive form of a complex function. The relationships involved include three transcendental sets of magnitudes. The first is the transcendental number *pi*, for rotation. The second is the transcendental, logarithmic number base, *e*. The third are the trigonometric functions most easily imagined by projecting a side view of the spiral from 3-dimensional space onto 2-dimensional space. The three kinds of transcendental numbers are obviously essentially the same, have a common origin, as of the same species, and are characteristic of the most elementary form of complex function possible. Furthermore, these are all defined without aid of arithmetic, by elementary methods of geometrical construction. Therefore, every school child of twelve or thirteen years of age ought to have mastered the fundamentals of the theory of a complex variable.

For reasons we shall explain, all functions of the species we have just described are called properly negentropic functions, and all processes properly described by such functions are called negentropic processes. All projections of such functions, as we have indicated the Archimedean spiral projection, are self-similar projections characterized by the Golden Section, as da Vinci, Pacioli, and, later, Johannes Kepler, insisted. Conversely, all such projections are reflections of negentropic processes.

Let us, next, imagine the projection of the circles we

There Are No Limits to Growth

defined, above, as the circles defined by each successive, completed, circular rotation of the spiral. The 2-dimensional projection is a nest of concentric circles with a common center. Now, the circumferences and areas of these concentric circles will be in harmonic proportion to one another. These harmonic proportions are the ideal (normal) proportions of growth-rates of human, animal, and plant populations, as determined by successive cycles of growth. This is, in first approximation, the significance of the term, "geometrical growth-rates."

There is therefore, no inherent reason that insofar as human wants require animal and plant populations, we cannot oblige animal and plant populations to grow geometrically at rates convenient to the rate of the human population growth, or even more rapidly. In fact, since the "agricultural revolution," this possibility has been demonstrated most conclusively.

"Whoa!" insist the Malthusians and Physiocrats in unison. "Ah! But what of the growth of mineral requirements? Have you not just admitted that da Vinci, Pacioli, and Kepler insisted, that 'geometrical growth-rates' of this sort are limited to living processes? What of the limitations imposed by mineral requirements?"

Look up to the stars, dear fellow! See that galactic spiral! Photograph it, if you do not trust the photographs astronomers have already produced in abundance. Now measure that spiral's harmonics geometrically. A Golden Section? You are shocked, angry? Are we saying that the universe as a whole is governed by a principle consistent with living processes? "That is hylozoic monism! I read about that in school, when I learned all about those pre-Socratic philosophers! What sort of ancient philosophical, unscientific double talk are you attempting to pass off on me?" Dear fellow, this is not new, nor something out of the pre-Socratic depths of scientific literature. Kepler founded modern mathematical physics, by proving that the harmonic composition of the solar orbits was uniquely determined in such a fashion that the harmonic aphelial-perihelial rates of planets and moons in their elliptical orbits depended upon the included principle of the Golden Section. "But, that is in contradiction to the Law of Conservation of Energy!" you exclaim.

Dear fellow, is it not your point that the universe as a whole, at least its mineral part, is governed everywhere by a Law of Entropy, in which negentropy is only exceptional? I see that you are nodding in agreement. Do you not prove by this so-called Law of Entropy that negentropic growth of mineral natural resources required for living processes is impossible? You shrug and nod at the same time: you agree generally, but you suspect me of being up to some trickery, and so you are becoming wary of committing yourself entirely to this point. Does this not tend to prove that the human population could not have increased by more than two orders of magnitude? "That is trickery. Now, you are being the Jesuit! It is only now that we are approaching those limits." Ah, but you agree with my description of your objection, with that condition you have just stipulated? Thank you; on that point, we are agreed.

Kepler and the Five Platonic Solids

During the lifetime of Plato, one among his collaborators, working at the Temple of Ammon in Cyrenaica, developed a proof, that only five varieties of regular polyhedral solids could be constructed in visible space (Euclidean space). Plato argued that this showed a limitation to the range of possible forms of existence visible in space, that there was some geometrical principle underlying visible space, which prevented any more than a limited range of geometrical forms from appearing within

There Are No Limits to Growth

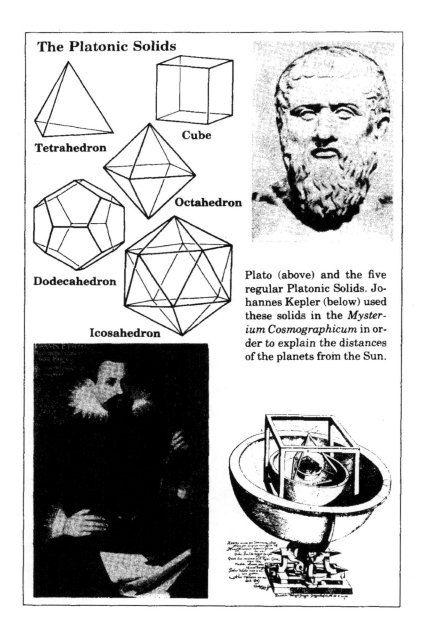

Plato (above) and the five regular Platonic Solids. Johannes Kepler (below) used these solids in the *Mysterium Cosmographicum* in order to explain the distances of the planets from the Sun.

The General Law of Population

it. For that reason, because of Plato's treatment of this, as a central feature of his *Timaeus*, these five kinds of polyhedral solids are known generally as the *Five Platonic Solids*.

Through aid of discoveries in geometry accomplished by Cardinal Nicholas of Cusa during the middle of the fifteenth century, Leonardo da Vinci's collaborator, Luca Pacioli, reconstructed a proof for the uniqueness of the Five Platonic Solids. The core of da Vinci's work on hydrodynamics, acoustics, his revolution in perspective (projective geometry), his study of biological processes and anatomy, and his theory of design of machines, were all centered on the combined work of Cusa and Pacioli on geometry, from this point of da Vinci's life's work onward. The combined work of Cusa and da Vinci to this effect was the basis for the development of mathematical physics by Johannes Kepler, and also the basis for the rigorous developments of geometry begun by a contemporary of Kepler's in France, Gaspard Desargues.

Kepler recognized that two leading features of his work on mathematical physics were much incomplete. For one thing, he outlined the specifications for development of a differential calculus. He also specified the need to perfect his theory of elliptic functions. Gottfried Leibniz completed the initial development of that differential calculus in a paper he submitted to a Paris publisher in 1676. Leibniz's success was based largely on the work in geometrical determination of differential arithmetic series of Blaise Pascal, a collaborator of Pierre Fermat, and follower of Desargues. Karl Gauss proved that Kepler's approach to elliptic functions was sound, and largely solved all the leading problems of elliptic functions.

The case of Isaac Newton has no bearing on the development of a differential calculus. Newton's design appeared a dozen years after Leibniz submitted his results

There Are No Limits to Growth

for publication, and though a chest of Newton's laboratory papers from that period survives, that chest contains no trace of work on a differential calculus. In any case, Leibniz's successful work on the differential calculus was known a dozen years before Newton's publication by members of the London Royal Society. Nonetheless, Newton's calculus is not even a good plagiarism. That calculus does not work, and is based on arithmetical series, with no bearing on the specifications of either Kepler or Leibniz respecting any of the essential principles involved.

The modern proof of the Five Platonic Solids is derived from a rigorous proof developed by Leonhard Euler, a follower of Leibniz, during the eighteenth century. Modern differential topology is more refined than Leibniz's analysis situs (the first form of modern topology) or Euler's topology, but the principled features remain the same.

The cumulative work of their predecessors in these directions was essentially completed by three German, mathematicians, Bernhard Riemann, Karl Weierstrass, and Georg Cantor, during the third quarter of the nineteenth century. In respect to fundamentals, all modern mathematical physics dealing with these matters today is referenced to the work of Riemann, Weierstrass, Cantor, and such immediate predecessors as Legendre, Gauss, and Dirichlet. Very little new has been accomplished concerning fundamentals since the third quarter of the last century.

So much, for the moment, of historical description. Now, we concentrate on the meat of the matter. How do we correlate living and mineral processes in terms of commonly underlying principles of physics? The work of Plato, Archimedes, Cusa, da Vinci, Kepler, and Leibniz settles all of the fundamentals in respect to principles. Moreover, as we shall show, the proof of the matter is elementary, not requiring a layman's trip through a

The General Law of Population

confusing maze of algebraic expressions.

The way in which Plato attacked the problem posed by the Five Platonic Solids was to inscribe the regular polygon corresponding to a side of one of these polyhedra within a circle. Plato treated the circumference of the circle as analogous to a string of a musical instrument, and focussed attention on the way in which a triangle, square, pentagon, and other figures divided the circumference into equal arc lengths. He argued that these divisions, as defined by the different polygons used, produced the same harmonic proportions as what we recognize today as the twelve-tone, octave musical scale. Kepler later repeated this construction as the elementary construction for his proof of the composition of the elliptical solar orbits.

Neither Plato's nor Kepler's harmonic values are precisely correct. The values of the well-tempered, 24-key polyphonic system of al-Farrabi, Bishop Zarlino, and J. S. Bach, are the correct values for mathematical physics. However, the correct values are obtained only through an elementary conical function, which neither Plato nor Kepler knew. Their results are a good approximation, nonetheless.

The problem of understanding Plato's reasoning in his *Timaeus*, until the work of Cusa, was that, until Cusa, medieval Europeans did not know the kind of geometry used at the Academy at Athens during Plato's time. Therefore, it was difficult to see why Plato should have imagined that anything could actually be proven by inscribing the polygons into circles. What connection did this have to the fact that only five species of regular polyhedra could be constructed in visible (Euclidean) space?

The leading cause for this problem was the influence of Aristotle. Although Aristotle's writings were unknown, except through Arabic commentaries, in Western Europe, until the middle of the thirteenth century, Greek geometry had been rewritten in Egypt under the influence of Aristotle's associates, the Peripatetics. Most of the geometry known to the Academy at Athens was completely rewritten in Egypt, in the form we know as the thirteen books of Euclid's Elements.

From the *Timaeus* itself, and from other sources, it is now proven, and conclusively so, that the principles of geometry rediscovered by Cusa, during the middle of the fifteenth century, were the same used by the classical Greeks of the Academy. This classical Greek geometry we know to have been very much like the program of *synthetic geometry* developed by Professor Jacob Steiner in Germany over the period of his work during the nineteenth century. This approach to geometry was the foundation of the scientific discoveries of Cusa, da Vinci, Kepler, Desargues, Fermat, Pascal, Leibniz, Euler, the Ecole Polytechnique under the leadership of Gaspard Monge and Lazare Carnot, of Gauss, Jacobi, Dirichlet, Riemann, Weierstrass, and Cantor. The elementary principles of this geometrical method are *principles of discovery*. Therefore, since these are elementary principles, they can be rather easily followed by intelligent laymen, without excursion into the complexities of the mathematical lattice-work of physics in detail. Moreover, as much as we have committed ourselves to prove here, can be proven adequately with nothing more than attention to those elementary principles of geometry.

This kind of geometry, synthetic geometry, is so named because it discards all of the axioms and postulates of Euclid's *Elements*, and proves everything by no other means than *proof by construction*. The most important feature of all such synthetic geometry is that the axiomatic (self-evident) existence of points and straight lines is thrown out of the textbooks. Only one kind of existence is assumed to be self-evident in all geometry, *the self-evident*

The General Law of Population

existence of the circle as an act of rotation.

What we have to say next is the hardest and most important part of all mathematical physics, and the most elementary: the fact that circular rotation is the only self-evident form of existence in visible space.

Figure 6, supplied by Dr. Tennenbaum, is a summary of the most fundamental theorem of what is called *differential topology*. All rigorous mathematical physics begins with a mastery of this elementary proof. It is a proof which is easily mastered by an intelligent child of thirteen years in any well-ordered educational institution. The leading points of the proof can be mastered by the reader now, with aid of reference to the figure and description which have been supplied.

As the figure shows, the entire proof depends only upon the action of folding. Folding is an act of rotation: the reader should bear that important point in mind. By comparing the areas associated, by means of folding, with half of the circumference of a closed action of rotation, we build a proof, which depends upon no assumptions of straightness or self-evident existence of points as *ontological* existences, that the circle is unique. It is the smallest act of closed rotation which may enclose a given area.

The next step is simpler. By folding a circle against itself once, we produce a line. We do not prove that this line is "straight;" the folding of a circle once against itself produces the diameter of the circle, which, by dividing the circle into two equal areas, corresponding each to a half-circumference, in that way, defines both the line and "straightness." No other definition of "straightness" is ever permitted in rigorous geometry and physics. Next, by folding the semi-circle against itself once, we define the

There Are No Limits to Growth

Figure 6
Fundamental Theorem of Differential Topology

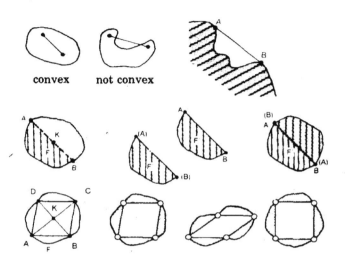

The Isoperimetric Property of the circle:
Jacob Steiner demonstrated, without use of any algebraic axioms, that the circle is that figure which encompasses a maximum area for a given perimeter. If it is assumed that another figure has been discovered which has this property, then this must at least be convex, for otherwise a connecting line could always be drawn from A to B which increases the area of the figure and decreases the perimeter. If the perimeter of a convex figure is divided into two parts of equal length, AB and BA, then the figure can be divided along the straight line which joins A and B. Assume that F is not the smaller of the two areas. If F is bisected and doubled through a rotation through 180 degrees around the median-line from A to B, then a symmetrical figure is produced with the perimeter of the original figure, but with possibly a greater area. In case the new figure is not convex, then that can be eliminated by application of the first construction step above. Now construct (as in the illustration) the points A, B, C, and D, and join them with straight lines. In case they form a rhombus inscribed within the figure, then the area of the figure can be increased through "straightening" of the rhombus into a square, without changing the perimeter. If this procedure is continued, then the figure will continually approach a circle, and the circle is the only figure which cannot be improved in this way.

The General Law of Population

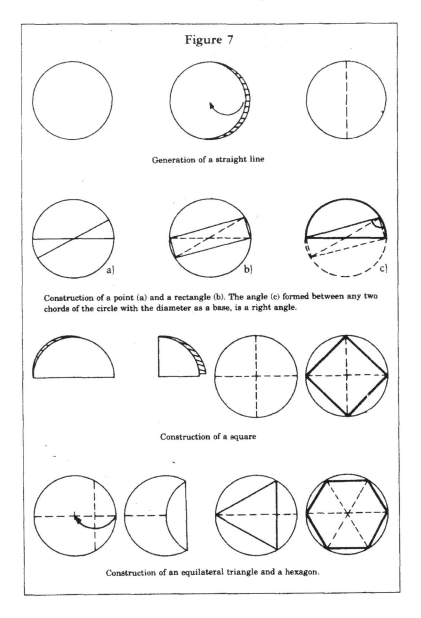

Figure 7

Generation of a straight line

Construction of a point (a) and a rectangle (b). The angle (c) formed between any two chords of the circle with the diameter as a base, is a right angle.

Construction of a square

Construction of an equilateral triangle and a hexagon.

center-point of the circle. This is the only definition of a "point" which can be permitted in rigorous geometry or physics.

The line and point, so defined, are the elementary *singularities* of the circle. They are, respectively, the first and second of the geometrical derivatives of the circle, whose existence depends upon the existence of the circle. No other definitions of "point" or "line" are permitted in rigorous geometry or physics. *The introduction of any added definitions, as axioms or postulates, leads to absurdities.*

The question of geometry ceases to be the paradox of Euclid's *Elements*, of how to measure the circle by means of axiomatically defined points and straight lines. The question of geometry becomes how to measure the line and point by means of the self-evident existence of the circle. *This is the foundation of all rigorous mathematical physics*, a fact whose rediscovery we owe chiefly to Cusa.

Beginning with nothing more than the circle and its primary singularities, we must construct everything using no added assumption introduced to "help" complete the construction. In that way, beginning with the derivation of the regular triangle, the regular square, and the regular pentagon, we must construct each figure using nothing but the circle and its singularities, plus figures we have constructed according to these principles of construction earlier.

Once we have covered the scope of the plane and solid geometry of visible space (Euclidean space), as fairly well mapped out by Euclid's *Elements* as to scope, we must proceed to derive the elementary principles of complex-domain geometry by means of construction of the conical form of self-similar spiral. Once we have done that latter, we begin the main mathematical side of physics work: we study the way in which constructions in the complex domain of complex, conical functions, project images into

The General Law of Population

the domain of plane and solid geometry of visible space. This notion of projective relations between a complex and visible *manifold* leads us to the elaboration of a field of mathematics associated with differential topology.

If people of Plato's time had anything approximating modern understanding of the geometry of the complex domain, no sign of this has turned up to the knowledge of the writer and his associates, *except in one very significant sense*, except in one sense which permeates Plato's references to the lawful implications of phenomena observed in visible space.

Plato insists that the world as our senses represent it to us is not exactly the real world, but a distorted image of the real world, the world seen only in the form of distorted reflections, as if distorting mirrors were everywhere embedded in the real universe.

The well-tempered keys are an excellent illustration of this point. Project a self-similar conical spiral onto the circular base of the cone. Since the characteristic of this projection is the Golden Section, the 3-space figure responsible for the projection has the characteristic features of the regular polyhedron associated with the regular pentagon. We divide the circular base of the cone into twelve equal sectors. The arc lengths of the arm of the spiral cut off by the radii dividing the circular base into twelve equal sectors, defines the proportions of the well-tempered, 24-key, twelve-tone, octave scale. This proves that those harmonic intervals, and also the intervals defined by the Platonic Solids (fifth, fourth, third) and their complements, *are the only natural musical scale and harmonics possible in the universe, existing before the first musician*. Any other tonal values are distortions. Any other principles of harmonic composition are not music. The question is: how well have musicians approximated recognition of the authority of those tonal values, how well have they practiced the principles that only such harmonic sequences exist for music?

The "distorted" images of sense perception are distorted in the manner implied by the case of the Five Platonic Solids. There is a bounding geometrical principle, which principle delimits what visible space can present as images to our senses. Whatever occurs in reality, reality will be distorted in such a way as to fit within the limitations of a geometrical principle of construction possible in visible space. This is the essential feature of what is sometimes termed "Platonic Realism": What we see is a distorted image of reality, analogous, broadly speaking to firelight shadows seen on the wall of a darkened cave. The shadows correspond to something real, but their form is not the real form of what they reflect.

Since only circular rotation is self-evident in visible space, *any limitations inherent in the attempt to make constructions in visible space, are limitations of what can be derived by construction from the circle*. Therefore, Plato was correct in insisting that the fact that only five kinds of regular solids could be constructed in visible space, signified that only the regular polygons corresponding to those possible kinds of polyhedra were characteristic of what could be constructed so from the circle as the point of origin.

In other words, the only *regular* crystalline structures which can be *universal* among processes in visible space are determined by a unique relationship between the circle and the derivation of the indicated regular polygons. That relationship reflects most directly the geometrically bounded form of possible existence in visible space. I

That is the original and correct meaning of the statement that our visible universe is *bounded but without limit, and yet also finite in some sense.*

The General Law of Population

The problem of mathematical physics is defined by this kind of proof, to be twofold. First, we must show how a geometry of the complex domain of complex functions produces the images of visible space, a projective connection which must be based on the harmonic principles adduced from the implications of the uniqueness of the Five Platonic Solids. Second, we must determine, with aid of mastery of the principled features of such a projective geometry, what kinds of experimental observations (depending upon phenomena of visible space) have the special quality of proving or disproving principled features of the geometry of the complex domain.

Beginning with Cusa's rediscovery of the principle of circular rotation, all of the progress of modern physics as to fundamentals, from Cusa through Riemann, et al., represents an elaboration of those two interrelated efforts.

The Principle of Least Action

Not merely is circular rotation the only self-evident form in visible space. *It is the only primitive form of physical action in space.* If an area represents the work accomplished, then the circular rotation which encloses such an area is the least action required to accomplish such work. That is the underlying principle of modern physics, *Leibniz's Principle of Least Action.* Although the principle is associated with Leibniz, it was already implicitly the principle of physics employed by Cusa, da Vinci, Kepler, et al. Synthetic geometry and physics are implicitly one and the same, inseparable subject matter.

This connection of geometry to physics is central to the issues of the law of population. The principle of least action is the only means possible for measuring technology. Hence, since the increase of mankind's potential relative population density is impossible without advances in technology, since even continued human survival in a civilized form is impossible without advances in technology, the measurability of technology is the central question of the law of population.

Although Leibniz has many precursors in this field, economic science, as economic science was known to the Founding Fathers of the United States, to the Ecole Polytechnique of Carnot, to Germany of the eighteenth and early nineteenth centuries, and so forth, was founded by Gottfried Leibniz, beginning his brief theses on the costs of productive labor of 1671, *Society and Economy*. It was Leibniz who defined the notions of *work* and *power*, as those terms apply to thermodynamics and economics today. On the same basis, Leibniz developed the conception of *technology*, called in eighteenth-century France *polytechnique*.

Leibniz's central point of reference for his establishment of economic science was his work on the subject of the heat-powered machine, by means of which, as he described the point, "one man can do the work of a hundred." The case of the operative employing such a machine, as compared with the case of the same operative producing the same kind of product without such a machine, enables us to associate the notion of "work" with such machines, and also the notion of power. However, there is also the case in which two machines consuming the same amount of coal for their power, are associated with different rates of work. This difference defines the root notion of technology.

The central feature of all machines is rotation, not only rotary motion as such, but the fact that all machine cycles are properly reduced by analysis to the equivalent of rotation. The heat power supplied to the machine is given new direction of action in space, and by changing the circumference of working-surface, as, by gears and cones,

The General Law of Population

we may increase the energy-flux density of continuous action way above the levels of the energy-flux density represented by the heat used to power the machine.

This principle of rotational action is maintained in the case of electromagnetic action. Any electromagnetic wave is a cylindrical approximation of a conical function of the sort we described earlier in the chapter. The sine-wave form of ideal electromagnetic radiation, such as electrical current or lasers or radio carrier waves, is typical of the point. This sine wave should be thought of as a spiral on a cylindrical surface, whose image has been projected from the 3-space of the cylinder, onto the 2-space of the cathode ray screen of the oscilloscope. It is a conical-functional form of self-similar spiral in which the negentropy is *apparently zero*--until we attempt to compress it against a barrier with which it is harmonically resonant in that state, at which point the quiet beam becomes most active, and does work.

The one area of work in which our geometrical notion is most poorly developed at present is the matter of work accomplished by chemical-process action, which we know to be ultimately electromagnetic, but have not sorted out these connections adequately. In these cases, we equate the chemical-process work done to its mechanical or electromagnetic equivalent, an arrangement which generally works quite well.

On principle, we equate all work-action to the principle of least action. We measure it as circular action work-equivalent, and understand that circular action in the visible domain is equivalent to harmonically-ordered conical action in the corresponding complex domain.

We do not measure heat power into a process as a quantity of calories when we come to the point of analyzing the technology of work. This must be the case since

There Are No Limits to Growth

technology measures different powers to accomplish work with the same quantity of kilowatt-hours of input. We compare, rather the apparent power of the input power to accomplish work *in that form* with the manifest power to accomplish work represented by the output.

It is the general case, as with production of industrial process-heat or electrical current, that the kilowatt-hours of output are substantially less than the kilowatt-hours of fuel consumed to produce that output. This will be a most unsatisfactory arrangement for economies, but for the fact that the power to do work of the output is greater, despite the fewer kilowatt-hours ostensibly embodied, than that of the input in form the input is supplied. It is not the quantity of heat which is critical for the power to accomplish work, but rather the *organization* of that heat power, the *physical geometry*, the technology of the output.

Despite the fact that it is the physical geometry of heat power which must be our primary focus, it is useful to define the problem to be solved by first stating the problem of society's need to accomplish work in terms of raw counting of kilowatt-hours of input and output of work in against work accomplished. We do so briefly now.

The usual procedure for examining a thermodynamical process is, first, to define what is meant by the usable energy throughput of the process, and, second, analyze that throughput in terms of two component functions of the flow. In the first instance we are restricting our definition of energy to something which changes in a manner of interest to us. This constitutes the adopted choice of physical phase-space for that study. Our next concern is to determine how much of the energy throughput must be consumed by the process itself, to the effect of preventing the process from running down, in the sense "running down" might be used for the case of the mainspring of a mechanical clock. If any energy throughput remains

The General Law of Population

available after such an *energy-of-the-system* requirement, we term the remainder the *free energy* of the process.

We then study the process in question, so defined, over a period of time, thinking in terms of a continuous process which may be examined in terms of successive cycles. We generally assume that the way in which the process will react to its own development over the interval studied will be governed by constant principles of physical behavior. That is the usual assumption for simple cases of continuous processes. We study this continuous process over successive cycles chiefly in terms of changes in the ratio of free energy to energy of the system.

A process in which *the free energy is negative*, or in which case the ratio of free energy to energy of the system is falling in a way which indicates the ratio will become negative, we usually describe as an entropic process. If this ratio is rising, we view the process as exhibiting "negative entropy," or *negentropy*.

The simplest way in which to represent a negentropic process, we have already indicated, earlier in this present chapter. The ideal representation of entropy is simply the reversed conical function. The matter becomes more complex, but these simplest, ideal cases, will be sufficient for our immediate needs here.

In the case of a society's economy, the energy of the system is the portion of all of the (physical) work done on nature by the society, up to the point of supplying everything needed to prevent the society's potential relative population density from falling. The useful work done in excess of that is ostensibly the free energy of the society's efforts, the net operating profit of the society, so to speak. The value of the free energy is the increase in potential relative population density effected by its "reinvestment" in the society.

There Are No Limits to Growth

This approach soon demonstrates itself to be useful, but not adequate.

Potential relative population density is expressed as a per capita value. It is expressed in this way for the total number of operatives effecting physical improvements in nature; it is also expressed for the labor force as a whole, including administration and services; it is also expressed for the population as a whole. All measurements are interrelated and relevant. In "reinvestments" of product produced into society, we are both expanding the population and its activities, and must be, at the same time, increasing the potential relative population density per capita.

At this point, the problem turns up. By increasing the per capita potential in this way, we are increasing the energy of the system per capita, if we assume a more or less fixed level of technology. The society will grow for a while, and then slip into an entropic phase: such cyclical expansion and collapse will appear to be inherent in the economy. As the ratio, per capita, of required energy of the system increases, under conditions of relatively fixed technology, the free energy ratio decreases. As depletion takes over, the economy and society plunge into collapse.

This can be overcome only on the condition that the capital goods produced by one hour of average labor today represent a higher level of technology than an average hour's worth of production of capital goods during the preceding cycle of production and reinvestment.

Therefore, once we recognize how deceptively cyclical a temporary rise in profitability of an economy may be, if the rate of technological progress is inadequate, we are obliged to recognize the direct connection between injections of improved technologies and maintenance of the potential relative population density. The measure of the output of

The General Law of Population

average labor is not the amount of goods produced, or the kilowatt-hours valuation of that output. The only proper measure is the amount of improved technology produced.

We must measure technology as negentropy. The conical function indicated earlier applies. The work accomplished by this negentropy is the negentropy per capita of the population. That defines the projectable concentric circles.

This means, that the aspect and form of human knowledge which corresponds to human survival is the kind of advance in technology which corresponds to such a negentropic function. This signifies the need for a succession of scientific breakthroughs, breakthroughs corresponding on principle to the higher hypothesis. The sustained survival of a society over a longer span, therefore depends upon the principle of discovery, the hypothesis of the higher hypothesis. *It is the perfection of the hypothesis of the higher hypothesis* which is the level of knowledge for practice at which human practice is congruent with human survival. *It is "at this level" that the cause and effect relationship between human activity and human survival is located.* It is at the "level" of knowledge that we improve the principles of discovery generating successive scientific revolutions, that man's activity is in correspondence to the efficient ordering of man's existence within the universe-- and on no lower level.

Let us suppose that no rigorous notion of such principles of discovery--the hypothesis of the higher hypothesis-- existed as efficient knowledge within a society. In that case, the society would probably fail to accomplish the next scientific revolution required for its continued existence. The society would therefore be on the pathway to "running down."

It is knowledge on this level, the level of the hypothesis

of the higher hypothesis, which correlates with man's mastery of the universe in such a fashion that human knowledge--this ruling knowledge--is congruent with continuously assured human survival. Therefore, no lesser definition of scientific knowledge is acceptable.

Since the universe responds to us continuously only to the degree that our willful practice is ordered by such an hypothesis of the higher hypothesis, that must be the efficient "level" of action directly corresponding to the lawful ordering of the universe. That constitutes conclusive empirical proof that it is on this level, and no lesser level, that mankind is enabled actually to know the lawful composition of the universe.

This was the standpoint from which Professor Bernhard Riemann elaborated mathematical physics' underlying principles of hypothesis. *It was this standpoint which Bertrand Russell hated with a deep, fanatical, irrational hatred.*

Relative to mathematics and mathematical physics, Russell's views and arguments are purely and simply absurd, and will seriously impair, if not entirely destroy the capacity for scientific work among those who tolerate viewpoints such as Russell's in their own thinking. Petty, envious, vindictive as Russell was, it was not the envy of a low-minded, nasty man which motivated his venom against Riemann, Weierstrass, Cantor, as well as Gauss and Professor Felix Klein. The issue was Riemann's moral conception of man in the universe, man as obliged to make himself a more perfect instrument of the Logos in the universe. Riemann was explicit on this point in some of the writings not published during his lifetime, but this viewpoint is clear to anyone familiar with the ABCs of scientific work in Riemann's famous 1854 habilitation dissertation, "On The Hypotheses Which Underlie Geometry," a work which Russell singled out for a wildly

The General Law of Population

irrational outburst in his own first published book.

Riemann showed in that 1854 publication what Gauss had already shown implicitly in his own discovery of the arithmetic-geometric mean, and in derivative work on elliptic functions.

Refer again to the conical representation of negentropic action. Focus on the volume of the cone which lies between the circular bases of two successive cycles of that conical action. From any point on the lower circle, cut a diagonal slice through that volume to the opposite point of the higher circle (Figure 8). This slice is an ellipse. The primary topological significance of the ellipse is that it has one more primary singularity than the circle. The action which produces negentropy has the effect of adding one singularity to the "system," from N to N + 1.

This implies that all action in the universe is implicitly negentropic, including the regular orbits of the solar bodies. This implication is congruent with the dominance of harmonic characteristics related to the Golden Section in astronomy generally, and to the derivation of all of Kepler's laws from the principles of solar harmonics which are, as a whole, congruent with that geometrical principle. This signifies that the time-direction of the universe as a whole is negentropic, directly opposite to the popular-science assumption that the universe is time-directed by entropy.

Just as that aspect of human knowledge which enables mankind to survive is characteristically negentropic, so the lawful ordering of the universe as a whole is indicated to be negentropic. Man, by his willful agreement with that lawful composition of the universe--by seeking willful agreement with the Logos, and by ordering his practice accordingly, masters the universe, becomes an instrument of the Logos, a conscious instrument of that Logos.

Figure 8

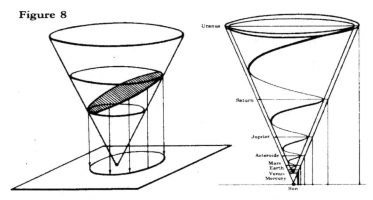

Right: Spiral model of the solar system. The orbits of the planets arose as shown on the left, out of projections of ellipses which lie between the circular conic sections depicted on the right.

Human life is sacred, and its increase is not only an expression of the universal law of the universe, but if man fails to bring his willful practice into agreement with that law, then the society so failing becomes unfit to exist, and will collapse, to make way, sooner or later, for one which fulfills the law. That is the Law of Population.

Giant development projects in the Third World nations, such as the Bhaka Dam (above), India's greatest dam, are as vital now as the exploration and colonization of space. Below, the lunar rover.

6

For Example, Britain's Positive Choice of Role

From the beginning of this book, we have stressed the view from man's standpoint in exploring and colonizing space. We have adopted this standpoint for several interrelated reasons. It has been possible to choose this point of reference, because man's exploration and colonization of space are implicit in the combination of existing technologies plus those in process of being introduced on a significant and growing scale during the decades immediately ahead. As we remedy the worst inequities among nations during the course of the decades ahead, the perceived purpose of human existence will appear to be the colonization of space, and this will become a rapidly growing view. At the same time, to lift our imaginations into space, from whence we look down upon the petty squabblings and other follies occupying the surface of our planet today, is to adopt an objective view of our present policies of practice, and so to adopt a larger, consciously critical view of the way we ordinarily think and behave.

From that vantage point in space, there is little which is more suited to arouse our scorn than some babbling barbarian who speaks of "national characteristics" as the biologically-determined traits of some particular portion of the human population.

There is only one differentiation of quality respecting political and related kinds of divisions within the human population as an entirety. That difference is "culture."

For Example, Britain's Positive Choice of Role

Some of the matters of difference commonly associated with use of the word "culture," are of no fundamental importance to us from a vantage point in space colonization. Such matters as differences in dietary customs, customs in clothing, and so forth, are of the sort an American, for example, expresses by referring to a "favorite Chinese restaurant"; we are broadened in our experience, and gratified, to explore other customs of this sort. The only truly significant differences in culture, the differences to which ideas of "rightness" or "wrongness" apply, are those cultural paradigms which express divergence in views of the meaning of man, of man acting in the universe.

There is only one human form of adversary to mankind, and that is a "wrong" variety of cultural paradigm. Nations express this "wrongness" by such means as warfare; at least one, perhaps both, represent the influence of a cultural paradigm which is adversary to mankind. Genocide, or merely bestial looting of a subjugated population, the practice of human slavery, racialism, and Malthusianism, are expressions of "wrong" cultural paradigms. The Khomeini insurrection in Iran is an expression of a "wrong" cultural paradigm, as was Nazism in Germany, or Fascism under Benito Mussolini in Italy, or the killing and raping practiced--according to Ilya Ehrenberg's Moscow propaganda instructions--against populations of the conquered adversary.

There are only two available courses of action against a "wrong" cultural paradigm. Either some agency must check it by force, or there must be a transformation in the culture of the indicated population. There is nothing "wrong" in the use of force, or imposed transformations in culture, in these cases, at least not merely because force is employed, or transformation induced. Such corrective actions are "wrong" only if an agency itself representing a "wrong" cultural paradigm conducts these actions, or if the new cultural paradigm imposed is itself "wrong."

Admittedly, what we are stating sounds rather "undemocratic" to many at first glance. The radical versions of "democracy" popularized today would judge the merits of Nazism as of 1936 or 1938, for example, by the question whether a majority of the eligible voters sincerely preferred Nazi rule, or would judge the "democratic authority" of a government perpetrating monstrous oppression against peoples abroad by the relative size of the popular support for that government at home. Similarly, today, persons argue for or against Malthusian policy proposals on the basis of the percentile of "popular opinion" which momentarily favors a view, no matter how immoral, and irreparable the cruelty perpetrated by the policies under debate.

Such notions of "democracy" are pure David Hume, pure Adam Smith, pure Bentham: the "pleasure" of the most numerous opinion, regardless of the consequences to mankind. Such "democracy," the irrational tyranny of the many, is aimed directly at the emergence of the tyranny of the few over the many, as in such cases as the tyrannies brought about by the Persian-financed "democratic party" of ancient Athens, or the Jacobin rule in France.

The tyranny of episodic opinion, becomes frequently of the opinion that a tyranny of the few is desirable. Since "pure democracy" is immoral by definition of principle, it usually leads to immoral consequences.

The principle of government must be the goal of a democratic republic *under law*. Yet, even this is no remedy for human afflictions administered by governments, or by consent of popular majorities, if the law itself is "wrong," expresses a "wrong" cultural paradigm in the form of law. It must be a democratic form of republican government

For Example, Britain's Positive Choice of Role

under the "right" law, a law expressing the "right" cultural paradigm. It must be a law, and government constrained by the sacredness of individual human life, and by the obligations of government to foster both the development of the individual's divine potentialities, and opportunities for the fruitful realization of those developed potentialities.

Men simply do not have the right, under proper constraint of law, to do to others whatever the majority of opinion wills. To argue to the contrary is itself evil, and a majority which does argue to the contrary is wicked on that account. We have the right, and obligation, to apprehend the murderer, to defend the nation against destruction, and so forth, often with fatal results. Yet, no one, no government, no popular majority, has the rightful authority to take life, or to ruin the condition of living of a single individual, except under those conditions and in those ways which are consistent with a law which regards the principle of sacredness of individual human life as beyond compromise. We can terminate human life only to preserve life, and we may terminate or consent to termination of our own lives for no other reason. We may kill in war only to defeat a tyranny, or a "wrong" culture, which can not be assuredly defeated in any other way. A tyranny or culture we oppose in war, or by related means, is "wrong" only if it rejects or grossly violates those principles concerning man, and man in the universe, which we are obliged to hold sacred.

We may use force rightly only to enable a "right" cultural paradigm to hold a "wrong" cultural paradigm in check, and may impose upon a people a culture "alien" to them only for this same reason, only by this same authority.

No, the views we propose are not rightly described as "undemocratic." It is the sacred rights of the individual we defend. The point is that the definition of "democratic" must never be separated from the issues of "right" and "wrong."

By definition, the proposal to impose any definitions of "right" and "wrong" upon societies incurs factional strife, and other difficulties. By whom, and by what means, shall "rightness" and "wrongness" be determined? It cannot be by any arbitrary authority. It cannot be the teachings of any church, merely because those are the teachings of a church, or because that church is traditionally embraced by a popular majority. No! In this matter, the "rightness" and "wrongness" of these churches' doctrines stand to be judged!

This does not signify that churches are either wrong, or superfluous, merely because they are churches. A religious mission of a church may bring individuals to the right course, and on that account the church which serves this purpose is to be admired. Moreover, science attests the existence of St. Augustine's and Plato's God, the God of Ammon and of Moses; the universe as an entirety, as a process of continuing, creative self-evolution, has the essential characteristics of a living being, and its manifest will, as the notion of the hypothesis of the higher hypothesis reflects the existence of such a Logos, is efficiently consubstantial with that universal, living being. Insofar as Christ expresses the essential part of love in bringing man's will into agreement with and service of the Logos, St. Augustine, and the *Gospel of St. John* are supported by the evidence of science. Cardinal Nicholas of Cusa comprehended these matters very well. On this account, certain religious doctrine, and the churches which embody that doctrine, have authority. With such matters, we have and offer no disagreement, nor with the importance of the individual's sense of personal connection and accountability to such a universal, living Being and the Logos.

The problem, in practice, is that those churches which

For Example, Britain's Positive Choice of Role

one might assume nominally to adhere to those principles, often repudiate them willfully or as a matter of neglectful practice. We dare not tolerate even the theocratic rule of a church which nominally adheres to a rightful teaching. The sacred book of the living Supreme Being is written in the universe, and all other books serve only as they guide us to read the universe aright, or as they are communication linking us personally to our greatest forebears and their work.

In the great family of mankind, now at the verge of venturing in common into the exploration and colonization of space, there are many religions. The law of nations, therefore, may be written only as an ecumenical law among those religions and religious cultures which share a common view of the sacredness of the individual human life, and a common view of the obligation to develop and unleash those fruitful potentialities for work which express the divine within the individual. In what book shall we read this ecumenical law? Upon what book of law shall we concur to adopt the law of nations? In what book shall we find written that which we are commonly obliged to agree is the distinction between "right" and "wrong"?

The writer agrees with the teachings of a number of religious denominations on matters which he regards as unshakably truths, essential for social practice. Yet, he will not be tempted opportunistically to place the relevant religious texts side by side, and suggest that those assembled make those texts common principles merely because the texts happen to concur. We have no right to make such a universal law, nor to propose it. We must prove before all men what is right and what is wrong. Nor need any religious adherent rightly fear this procedure, unless he fears that his own religious belief is provably wrong.

It is comforting for one of Western civilization, like this

writer, to stand upon the injunction of the Book of Genesis, that mankind must be fruitful and multiply, and fill the earth and exert dominion over nature and everything within it. With that, he, like many, fully concurs. It is comforting to stand with the Gospel of St. John, with the missionary writings of St. Paul, or to stand with Cardinal Nicholas of Cusa on the issues of the Council of Florence, on the premises of *De Non Aliud*, and the ecumenical *De Pace Fidei*, or to stand, in ecumenical fraternity with Philo of Alexandria and ibn-Sina's *Metaphysics*. It is also comforting to sit with great Sanskrit scholars. Yet, this is not sufficient. We must prove the law, the law of "rightness" and "wrongness" before all mankind, and we must prove it by the heavens themselves. We owe much to these books, those who wrote for them, and those who lived by them. Yet, we owe them enough to have learned something from them, from the history of mankind's struggle to master the lawful composition of this universe as a whole. In that history, and the principles we may adduce from it, there is the written law of the heavens, the heavens which mankind is about to enter.

That Book of Genesis--the book of life--has enjoined us to increase the potential relative population density of mankind. We have, with some backsliding and reluctance, obeyed that injunction thus far, to the point of increasing the potential relative population density of mankind by more than two orders of magnitude above that possible in man's primitive condition. In the progress of that labor which the same book enjoins us is our fate, we have made successive scientific revolutions, and have been enabled thereby to discover that there is a common principle of discovery which efficiently orders the succession of such revolutions, a principle of discovery whose exact nature admits of perfection in our knowledge. It is this principle, this power, which expresses that which distinguishes us above the beasts, the potentiality within us which is divine.

For Example, Britain's Positive Choice of Role

Figure 9

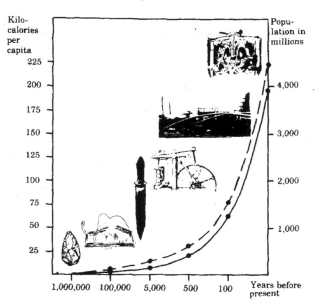

Time line showing the principal periods of human history. Paleontological history, from 2 or 3 million years ago to about 5,000 years ago, was characterized by stone tools and gradually improved methods of hunting and gathering of food. In Archeological history, beginning about 5,000 years ago, the agriculture of the Bronze Age was developed. In the remaining 2,500 years or so before the present, the introduction of fossil energy sources and atomic energy has increased the relative potential population density by three orders of magnitude.

Our clear and proven duty is to perfect that knowledge, not merely for the material advantages it affords us, but for the sake of that perfection itself. In the final analysis, the purpose of knowledge is not that of serving our material wants, but rather progress in satisfying those wants has the purpose of guiding us, through our labor, to perfection of our knowledge, to a state of increasing agreement with the Logos.

In each thing we do, whether in that labor by which we live, or in the matter of judging the law, we must yearn to accomplish a further perfection of our knowledge of the principle which we have named the notion of the hypothesis of the higher hypothesis. The Logos is the law of this universe, *the natural law*. It is in the book of the Logos that we must read the law before all men. It is time to turn the next page.

In this sense, technological progress is the law.

Plato, St. Augustine, and Dante Alighieri

The objection is posed: "Technological progress has not proven efficient in obliging its users to become moral." It is notably true, that providing a professional assassin with an improved weapon may improve his professional scores without showing any beneficial change induced in his morality.

It is nonetheless true, that the individual experience of technological progress, at least as the shared experience of populations, does correlate with increased value attached to rational forms of thought and social behavior. Wherever populations have become more rational in this fashion, they have become perceptibly more moral. The converse is more emphatically true. Technological pessimism, whether through stagnation in technological progress, or through lack of access to it and its benefits, promotes cultural pessimism. Such cultural pessimism, in turn, more or less invariably unleashes all of the devils which a population is capable of becoming; the Nazi case is exemplary of this. Similarly, the most efficiently degrading thing a nation can do to some among its population, is to assign them to suppressing technological progress, by such means as "colonial operations," among another people, an occupation which promotes the most degraded views of man--both of oppressed and oppressor--among those so engaged.

For Example, Britain's Positive Choice of Role

Yet, although it is incontestable that technological progress is morally as well as materially beneficial-- if it is technological progress as we have defined it in the preceding chapter, this fact does not answer all of the various points implied by the cited objection. We must consider upon what technological progress acts to encourage moral advancements, and by means of what kinds of processes this is accomplished.

For that, we turn our attention to a matter most famously treated, successively, by Plato, by St. Augustine, and by the *Commedia* of Dante Alighieri: the fact that the possible moral conditions of mankind occur on three alternate levels, corresponding, approximately, to Dante's "Inferno," "Purgatory," and "Paradise." These three levels of morality are the alternatives natural to the human social condition in general, and are therefore the primitive root of the individual's potential to generate and to assimilate cultural paradigms. It is upon these processes that the experience or absence of technological progress acts, to influence the development of moral outlooks (cultural paradigms) in an upward or downward direction.

We are all born into a "state of original sin." We are born irrational hedonists, yet also possessed of that spark of the divine by means of whose development we may overcome the morally degraded condition into which we are born. All evil in society is the product of an abortion of the process of development out of such infantile irrationalistic hedonism, or the regression of the child, youth, or adult, to such an infantile condition.

The essential feature of the moral philosophy of Thomas Hobbes, John Locke, David Hume, Adam Smith, Jeremy Bentham, and John Stuart Mill, for example, is that they are essentially morally infantile. The infantile mind is obsessed with "What I want," and oblivious to the broader implications of that action for society generally. This is the essence of anarchism, existentialism generally, and the philosophical root of the character of the individual Nazi. This is Dante's "Inferno."

This feature of David Hume so offended Immanuel Kant, that Kant wrote several books of extensive impact to refute what Kant abhorred as Hume's immoral quality of "philosophical indifferentism." Kant summed up the matter in the last section of his *Critique of Practical Reason*, the "Dialectic of Practical Reason." The definition of the determination of morality in the individual occurring in that location presents a conception of man which is more or less exactly the state of man in Dante's "Purgatory."

Kant argues that society acts upon the infantile mind, to, as Sigmund Freud might wish to argue, "repress" those features of infantile impulses which are socially undesirable in their consequences. To the degree the individual's love of parents and society is associated with such "acts of repression," the attachment of lovingness to the experience of the "repression" prompts the individual to associate a positive quality to the "repression." So, the "negative" quality of the "repression" is negated by its association with love, and the individual prides himself in the changes in impulses so accomplished. By such "negation of the negation," the individual identifies himself as *a moral person*. He will do nothing whose consequences are known to be asocial, at least, not without a bad conscience suffered in the process.

Kant is not notably associated with the emotion of lovingness, but is notably dry of such manifestations in personal life and in writings. We may be accused of having added something to Kant on this account; we would say that we have *corrected* Kant on this account.

Kant's quality of dryness came to the attention of Friedrich Schiller, who emphasized the deficiencies bearing

For Example, Britain's Positive Choice of Role

upon poor, dry old Kant's inability to grasp the active principle of great artistic composition. Kant was a bright old fellow, with the particular merit of being consistent even when he was laboring in service of an erroneous assumption. Kant has the merit of driving his assumptions to their uttermost limit, and reporting frankly what he encounters in so doing. His *Thing-in-Itself* and his candid report of his struggles with *a priori synthetic knowledge*, are illustrations of his candid thoroughness. One fears that poor old Kant, when he died, not only arrived in Purgatory, but has stubbornly refused to leave that place since. The fellow believed that Paradise existed, but also insisted that there is no *logical way* in which a person might enter it. Kant admires the idea of Paradise, but he wouldn't enjoy the place; the writer's advice to St. Peter, if advice were asked, would be to leave Kant in Purgatory, where the customs and climate are agreeable to the old fellow's notoriously habituated nature.

In point of fact, what Kant circumscribed with the words "a priori synthetic knowledge" not only exists, but is accessible to human conscious knowledge on principle. It has the form of the notion of the hypothesis of the higher hypothesis. We turn our attention to the view of the matter in the setting of Kant's predicament, and then examine the same matter from the standpoint of Schiller's professions of poet, classical dramatist, and historian. This inquiry has the relevance of dealing not only with Kant's inability to enter Paradise, but with a similar difficulty commonplace among most moral persons in society generally.

In the current of mathematical physics we have summarily outlined earlier, we begin in geometrical physics with only a single principle of action in the universe. This single principle of action has the form (relative to our image of visible space) of being circular rotation, as the isoperimetric first theorem of differential topology defines circular rotation. *The first rotation creates the universe out of nothing*, by defining a circular plane by no yardstick but the circular action itself. There is no notion of the definition of a plane before that, and no metric to state how large or small the circle might be.

This action is the first definition of physical space. We have introduced a *limitation* into the formless, measureless void of space. Now, we perform the same action upon the circle we have created, and so create the "straight line," which is defined as the self-halving of the plane created by the original act of creation. We have now introduced *a second limitation* into the universe as a whole. We perform the act of rotation upon the original circle a second time: we so create a point, the *third limitation* imposed upon what was originally a formless, measureless void.

We proceed so, to create the universe in detail. We may never employ anything but that we have created out of the original principle of action.

We remind ourselves as we proceed, that we are not The Creator. We are thinking *creation*, and defining *creation* as the only action possible in a *created* universe. Yet, we are only thinking about creation; we did not create the universe. Once we have reminded ourselves of this important fact, we become physicists. We compare our *thinking creation* with the creation which exists, of which we are part. We study what exists as *a process of creation*, and measure our principle of creation as a process against the real creation.

In that enlightened state of mind, we strike upon the Platonic Solids. In the center of those Platonic Solids is the pentagon: everything which is possible in created visible space hangs upon the relationship of the dodecahedron to the pentagon's derivation from the circle. (See Figure 10 for the dependency of the other four Platonic Solids upon

For Example, Britain's Positive Choice of Role

Figure 10
Producing the four other Platonic Solids from the dodecahedron. If a diagonal is drawn through each pentagonal face of the dodecahedron, a cube is produced (a). Proceeding in the same way, a tetrahedron can be produced from the cube (c). If the midpoints of the faces of the dodecahedron are joined, an icosahedron (b) is produced, and in the same way, an octahedron can be produced from the cube (d).

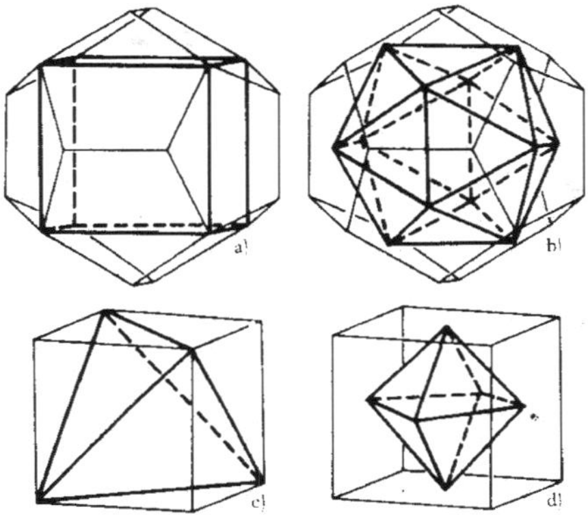

the dodecahedon.)

However, this geometrical boundedness of visible physical space shows us that visible space is a distorted reflection of reality. We are led to the conical functions in a complex domain, which account fully for the harmonic features and other apparent properties of visible physical space. In this domain, the continuous domain of the complex conical functions, everything is directly consistent with the single principle of creation, which we have elected to name the principle of least action. This proves, experimentally, to conform to the lawful way in which the actual Creator has organized the universe. We know that we have struck rightly upon the basic features of the principle of creation employed by the Creator. Now, we have learned how to begin to read some of the introductory chapters of the great book the Logos is writing in the heavens.

We have begun to enter Paradise, on condition we understand exactly what it is we are engaged in doing.

There Are No Limits to Growth

The principle of creation, this conceptualization of creation, in which action in the universe is itself action of creation, is therefore a knowable principle. Moreover, implicitly, by mastering this principle, we can create, on condition that we follow the way in which the Creator practices creation. We desire to become the instruments of the Creator by mastery of this principle, and by mastery of the sense of direction which He has embedded in his creation. When this becomes our pleasure, we have entered through the portals into Paradise.

Kant was wrong on this matter.

The essence of composing classical poetry and drama, or the comprehension of universal history, is thinking about conscious thought in a definite way. The object of this thinking about conscious thinking, in which conscious thinking becomes the object of conscious thinking, is to understand why we (and others) think as we can be observed to do. Insofar as we adjust the object of such reflections in terms of the practical consequences to which decisions lead, we are enabled to isolate in our own thinking those assumptions which characteristically underlie the kinds of decisions provably disastrous for society or merely for ourselves. As in rigorous examination of underlying assumptions of prevailing science, preparatory to effecting a scientific revolution, we willfully change the embedded assumptions of our own ordinary decision-making, to make ourselves better people..

The most concentrated expression of such conscious thinking about conscious thinking is classical drama of the sort typified by Aeschylus, Shakespeare, and Schiller himself. In the case of Schiller, his later tragedies were based on a thorough study of history. Although he employed dramatic liberty to alter history upon the stage, all of the issues and problems of behavior placed upon the stage were faithful to history, were actual problems of

For Example, Britain's Positive Choice of Role

history, were concentrated expression of real tragedies of leaders and peoples in real history. Thus, each of his great tragedies is congruent with the principle of higher hypothesis. Moreover, in addition to being the most beloved and influential poet and dramatist of Germany during his lifetime, into approximately 1850 or so, Schiller was a political leader, the *primus inter pares* of the Weimar Classic circle which included Goethe, Kant, and the young Wilhelm von Humboldt among its participants. More than anyone after Leibniz, Schiller shaped the reforms unleashed by Stein, Humboldt, and Scharnhorst in 1809-1813. His dedication, especially after the horrifying spectacle of the Jacobin Terror in France, was to ensure that in the German people the great moment of the eighteenth-century, produced by the leadership of Leibniz and Franklin earlier, would not find, as it had in France, the tragedy of a "little people." Although the Hohenzollern betrayals of Germany from the 1815 Congress of Vienna onward, plunged the German people into frustration and the cultural pessimism of Romanticism, Schiller's dramas, especially, shaped much of the German people in 1809-1815 into a great people, one of the noblest, rapid shifts in the cultural paradigm of a people accomplished in modern history.

In Schiller's devastating criticism of poor Kant's sterile misconception of aesthetics, Schiller describes the creative principle energizing great art to an effect which is congruent with the notion of the creative principle we have described above.

So, we identify the double aspect of the person who has attained Paradise. His intellectual pleasure of his labor, is to comprehend the creative principle and to serve that principle in the universe actively, in service of the principled form and direction given to continuing creation by the Creator. This intellectual character of his pleasure must be energized by a great love for humanity, of the

There Are No Limits to Growth

character illustrated by Schiller's efficient, creative love for the moral condition of the German people. Without these two qualities, intermingled, and intermingled with a sense of personal service and accountability to the Creator in the same loving way, there can be no entry into Paradise.

To love, is to labor to bring humanity into Paradise, and by nothing other than the exercise of these means.

That is the great book of law which the Logos is continuing to write in the heavens. That is the law we must read to the peoples of this planet, that those peoples may prepare themselves morally to enter the heavens, and that they may not destroy one another and themselves in the effort to reach the point of launching the great exploration.

This has many approximations in everyday life. One person builds something, to be given as a present to another, and constructs it to have some feature which is better than any such object of the same sort he knows to exist. He delights in the pleasure he will give to the recipient, and delights in those capacities upon which he draws to effect this innovation.

A well-composed poem, which expresses the same principle of result and design, is another illustration. A musical composition satisfying the same principle is the characteristic of the greatest composers. The great composer separates himself or herself from "professional recognition" for its own sake--he is never a mere entertainer, seeking success as an entertainer. There must be a moral principle served: a gift of some usefully ingenious feature, a struggle to expand the power of musical composition. There is love, the search for truth along the frontiers, the risk involved. A good drama is written not to entertain, but to ennoble people in an entertaining way, and to measure ennoblement by the desire to bring them into Paradise, as Schiller's dramas exemplify

For Example, Britain's Positive Choice of Role

this.

Since the power of composing music has become in fact a lost art during this century, it is appropriate to select this work of Paradise as an example of the manner in which creative principles enter directly into all the essential features of well-tempered polyphony. As we shall now show, the differences in interpretation of theories of musical harmony and composition, insofar as these pertain to persons "literate" in the use of music as a form of language, are ultimately only differences in morality. Wherever a music-theoretical difference occurs, the source of that difference is not musical per se, but reflects a moral difference in the person choosing that musical-theoretical view which coincides with the morality of his personal world-outlook at that time.

Music begins with the well-tempered tonal domain of polyphony to which we referred earlier. There is only one set of musical tonal values and harmonic relationships possible within creation, the well-tempered values, determined by the principle of the Platonic Solids, as defined by the conical function we indicated earlier. Those values existed as the only musical values of tone and harmonics before the first musician existed.

In fact, we know that well-tempered values were adopted at the time of Plato, and, therefore, possibly earlier. They were specified by the ninth-century Islamic scientist al-Farrabi, who writes that the well-tempering he employed for his twelve-tone, octave scale was already very ancient at that time. There are circumstantial reasons for believing that the well-tempered system was understood and used by Leonardo da Vinci, together with the bel canto method of voice-training and singing already in use at that time. The well-tempered principles were taught by the sixteenth-century Bishop Zarlino, who is the only known modern

Figure 11
Kepler's derivation of the musical intervals.

Since the Greeks (Pythagoras), it has been known that a musical interval between two notes produced by a vibrating string is determined by the ratio of the lengths, assuming an equal tension on the strings.

The ratios determined by the Greeks were as follows:

$$\left.\begin{array}{ll}\text{Octave} & 2:1 \\ \text{Fifth} & 3:2 \\ \text{Fourth} & 4:3 \\ \text{major Third} & 5:4 \\ \text{major Sixth} & 5:3\end{array}\right\}\text{"Prime" intervals}$$

$$\left.\begin{array}{ll}\text{minor Third} & 6:5 \\ \text{minor Sixth} & 8:5\end{array}\right\}\text{Derived intervals}$$

Example of Pythagoras' Principle
In order to produce a D note on the G-string of a violin, the fingers must be placed so that the vibrating section of the string is ⅔ of the original length. Kepler derives these ratios geometrically from the Platonic Solids. If a string is made into a circle, then the lengths corresponding to the fifth, fourth, and the major third are determined by the faces of the Platonic Solids inscribed within the circle. The faces are the triangle, square, and pentagon.

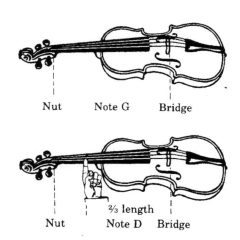

Nut   Note G   Bridge

⅔ length
Nut   Note D   Bridge

For Example, Britain's Positive Choice of Role

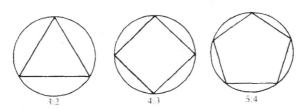

These figures are "prime" and correspond to the arithmetical prime numbers, since no regular polygon is contained within them. The hexagon is not a prime figure since it contains a regular triangle.

From the other consonant intervals, the major sixth is obtained from the pentagon, while the minor third and the minor sixth are derived from the hexagon and the octagon. The hexagon and the octagon are derived through doubling of the triangle and the square (below).

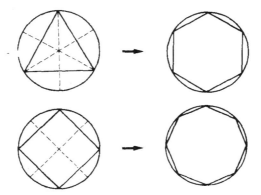

Kepler explains the fact that the other ratios such as 7:6 are dissonant in music because the corresponding polygons do not correspond to faces of Platonic Solids and are not constructible by means of a straight edge and a compass.

There Are No Limits to Growth

music theoretician to deal with fundamentals; all musical theory to date is dependent upon the work of Zarlino--otherwise, everything, extant in the name of musical theory as to fundamentals is merely approximation or, in most instances, somewhat less than of scientific merit.

The requirement of the 24-key well-tempered domain is derived from implications of the Platonic Solids. The principle of harmonic progression in music is based on the fifth, fourth, and third, and their complements. That is, the fifth, fourth, and third, are the geometrical equivalent of "prime numbers;" they cannot be reduced to regular polygons of a lesser degree geometrically by halving. By doubling the "prime figures," we obtain the sixth (hexagon), eighth (octagon) and tenth (decagon). So forth, and so on.

Music is characterized by development, prosodic (from music's dependence on poetry, as we shall indicate) and harmonic. Harmonic development is a lawful key progression governed by either a prime or secondary harmonic interval, or by the occurrence of a polyphonically-determined dissonance, which must be resolved by composition. Dissonances are a special singularity, which must be resolved in the sense Dirichlet's principle defines resolution topologically. The 24-key domain "behaves" as a potential-surface within which resolution consistent with Dirichlet's principle occurs.

There is no vertical harmony in music, except as vertical harmony is created-in much the same sense a line is created in geometry. There are no laws of vertical harmony, that is to say, even though many musicians who do not understand deeper principles may argue to the contrary through false impressions or acquired habits. All harmony in music is horizontal, is time-directed, not vertical. Each line of polyphony consists of the equivalent of one singing voice, which, except in the case of unfortunate freaks suited to

For Example, Britain's Positive Choice of Role

perform in carnivals and circuses, cannot sing two notes at the same time. Polyphony occurs through the introduction of a second singing voice, which enters (in canonical basic harmonics) in time sequence and harmonic sequence, following the preceding note in the first voice.

In other words, at the note before the second canonical-voice is introduced, the first singing voice branches, continuing in its own voice-line while also branching to, forming a sequence with, the second voice-line's first voice. Thus, this consonance with the two notes, the following note in its own voice-line and the first note of the second voice-line, determines a vertical consonance.

This principle of branching, or across-voice sequences, is extended throughout the composition.

In actual musical compositions, the apparent result may differ in form. The composer may open with chords, and so forth. However, the composition as a whole is derived from musical root-conceptions which are expressible in the form of canons. That is, by striking a chord at the opening of a composition, one is posing a question: How did that chord come into existence? What canonical analysis accounts for the horizontal determination of that vertical array?

This involves merely the harmonics of composition. Music is essentially an outgrowth of sung poetry, whence music derives its metrical features. Muslc is polyphonic poetry, which, by being polyphonic, requires submission to harmonics in the choice of tonal values for the syllables of the poetic line. The choral polyphony which is the essence of music is abstracted from the sung poetry, to provide instrumental polyphony.

That is the direction of development of music through Ludwig van Beethoven, as underscored by the across-voice polyphony of the late string quartets--which oblige the performer to phrase not only his instrument's voice, but to cooperate with the other performers--often enough--in phrasing a voice defined across the instruments. It is the problems requiring resolution, arising from setting metrically defined voices which are consonant in themselves in polyphonic configuration, which is the heart of that part of music which makes music music: development. A classical musical composition is a polyphonically sung poem, in which the unit-composition as a whole is defined by a unifying, single line of completed development. That development is the "musical idea" unique to the composition. This development is simultaneously harmonic (within the 24-key manifold) and metrical..

So, classical well-tempered polyphony presents exactly the same kind of problem in creative work as scientific discovery. Its function is, predominantly, to celebrate as music the kinds of creative potentialities within the mind of the performers and listeners which are otherwise the means for all forms of creative work, for embrace of the principle of the hypothesis of the higher hypothesis. Therein lies the importance, the sacredness of great musical composition.

The destruction of the power to compose and to hear music as music was initially chiefly the doing of Franz Lizst, Richard Wagner, and other exponents of the Romantic school. It is exemplary of confusion produced, that musicologists purport to discover Romantic features of Beethoven, and class Brahms in the same collection with his bitter adversary, Wagner. They hear no difference between the "classical" and "Romantic" music, but only a "certain sound," a "certain style."

The "classical school" is not a "sound" or a "style," it is a principled view of man and man in nature expressed as musical composition. Rameau, for example, was a true Romantic. The true "classical composition," exemplified

For Example, Britain's Positive Choice of Role

by the cases of J. S. Bach, the post-1782 Wolfgang Mozart (emphatically), and Beethoven, is based on the principle of lawful development only, and creativity (development, etc.) as limited to lawful discoveries. The Romantic school adopted as its principle "pleasing effects" produced by clusters of sounds, the "soaring effect" of arbitrary chromatic progression, and so forth. This was not new to the nineteenth century; it was already the principle of practice of Claudio Monteverdi, a former student of Zarlino's hired by Venice to attempt to destroy Zarlino's influence with such Romantic policies of composition.

The essential feature of the various schools which have destroyed music among composers and in the minds of audiences (and numerous performers and conductors), are all based on violating systematically those principles of well-tempered polyphony associated with the implications of the Platonic Solids. A purely arbitrary effect, which solves no rigorously defined problem, is mistaken for "creativity," in the nonsense-music of Schoenberg, for example. Arbitrary sensual effects are the typical alternative to the "intellectual modernists." Sometimes something of both is combined. So, performers perform nothing but gibberish for the edification of audiences, who hear music as they read a crossword puzzle on a subway ride to work; trying to "make sense of it," passes for aesthetic "appreciation." Or, if one tires of it, one may descend into the purely bestial dionysiac rhythms of the rock concert.

The rock concert, the Romantics, and the "modernists" are the denizens of the "Inferno." The passable composition, as passable music school exercise in imitation of the classical mode, like the mere restatement of a previously solved solution to a problem of development by a serious composer, brings us to the level of Immanuel Kant's "Purgatory," while a breakthrough in principles of development, such as we are accustomed to associate with Beethoven's breakthroughs in composition, is the standpoint of "Paradise."

The "Purgatorian" of today is usually a competent performer, who is astonished that he cannot compose despite his supposed mastery of interpretation. Listen to the principles he employs to explain interpretation, and you learn at once why he cannot compose classical compositions. He has rejected the rigorous standpoint--the synthetic geometry-like standpoint--on which classical composition depends. He is too much concerned with what "it should sound like," and overlooks the matter of rigorously defined musical ideas.

The general principle, by which technological progress affects the potential shifts in morality from one of the three levels to another, is that our ideas and morality are centered in relationship among persons in society. This relationship has two interdependent aspects to be considered here. First, *there is the matter of how we value other persons.* Second, is *the way in which we define the common purpose to which the activities of the individual members of society are directed in terms of concerted effect.* It is as the principle of technological progress affects the latter, that the practical value of other persons is defined for us.

In a society in which no technological progress occurs, the lack of such progress imposes a beast-like quality of "traditional" modes of social practice. It is as we perceive ourselves to depend upon the creative powers of others, that we value others for their creative powers of mind. It is only in this circumstance that the members of a society generally view one another as human. This latter condition is characteristic of those societies whose populations are defined "moral," in the Kantian sense. In Purgatory, we recognize that human qualities of creative mental powers are necessary for discovery and assimilation of advances in

For Example, Britain's Positive Choice of Role

technology, and recognize that our well-being depends upon this, and also upon rational behavior from other persons in matters of common affairs in society generally.

What is desired, is to shift this further: to cause technological progress to be valued as the indispensable means for the development of the creative powers of mind, rather than viewing the development of the powers of mind as a means for obtaining the material benefits of technological progress. Once love for the development of other minds prompts one to promote technological progress as the general form of social practice agreeable to that development of the minds of oneself and others, then one is approaching the gates of Paradise.

Conversely, we drive people away from the gates of Paradise as we adopt a policy of educational practice which states that we educate the young only for their destined adult occupations of employment and so forth. If we deprecate technological progress in practice and in word, such a general opinion can drive any population from Purgatory into the existentialist immorality of the Inferno.

The Required Policy--In General

There are two policies on which we must become agreed, if we have the quality of love which can lead us ourselves into Paradise. First, we must resolve upon increasing the potential relative population density of mankind as a whole, by mobilizing advanced--and advancing--technology, as it is available, to lift the majority of mankind out of the threatened condition into which post-war economic policies and present economic collapse have pushed it. Let us resolve to dedicate the next two generations to ridding this planet of virtually every vestige of inequity on this account. Second, we must, at the same time, adopt a higher, common purpose for mankind: the exploration and colonization of space, for whatever higher purpose we later discover this to lead mankind.

The function of this twofold resolution is to direct the policies of practice of mankind, and our shared consciousness of purpose for that practice, to the effect of inducing a general view of man, and of man in the universe which converges upon the moral condition of Paradise.

Malthusianism, and the wicked cultural paradigms it reflects must be extirpated from the practice of nations immediately, by whatever means of force of law are required to accomplish that result immediately. *Malthusianism has no rights as a political opinion under natural law*; it is to be treated as the practice of any other form of crime, and its advocacy recognized as expression of criminal mentality. Those people whom the Malthusians would cause to die, have a right to live, and no Malthusian, for any reason, has a right of one second's duration, to deprive them of life, nor the right to campaign to induce them to accept death willingly by various methods of news media and other brainwashing. Euthanasia, even with the consent of the victim, is murder, a capital offense, especially if the consent is induced by social pressures brought to bear.

Yet, we cannot be content with the *force of law*, any more than we are content to merely imprison a growing population of drug users and drug sellers. We must uproot the evil practice from the perpetrators' dispositions. We must alter the culture, the cultural paradigms of the potential perpetrators of crimes and other wrongs. We must engage in "cultural engineering." We must impose scientific and technological progress as inalterable policies of states and relations among states, in order that human beings may be morally human, that the natural law may be served by and for the benefit of each human individual.

For Example, Britain's Positive Choice of Role

In these pages, we have referred most concretely to the moral responsibilities of leading circles of Britain and the United States' Eastern Establishment for such crimes as the African slave-trade, the China opium-trade, and complicity in the wickedness accomplished with aid of the Pugwash Conference. It is fitting to close these pages with statement of a hopeful look toward Britain.

Those of Britain and the United States (among those of other nations) who have fostered the Pugwash Conference and what it represents, have brought us to the edge of possible general thermonuclear warfare, and to the possibility, otherwise, that either civilization collapses before the unleashed four Horsemen of the Apocalypse or under world-empire dominated by the Soviet state. These outcomes would be calamities for themselves, as well as for humanity generally.

Now, the time has come, in the course of these events, that the United States, Britain, and other nations must awaken to the growing, immediate perils of the situation. They must rebuild their economies, and summon to this purpose the most advanced of the available technologies available today and during the immediate future. We may hope, therefore, that this mobilization of most the world's economy, and implicitly all, will not be a precursor of early general warfare. We may also hope that the uplifting of the human mind and morals in the nations affected will not be again a temporary advancement in sense of human purpose. We may hope that the benefits of response to immediate peril will endure beyond the immediate crisis, that we shall all have learned something from reflection on the process by which we brought ourselves into such peril, and will be therefore desirous of changing ourselves, to rid ourselves of those assumptions of principles of pleasure and pain which have degraded us as peoples while leading us to the edge of catastrophe.

There Are No Limits to Growth

Let us persuade one another, as persons and nations, to perform the indicated "cultural engineering" upon our society, that we may adopt as universal law of practice among nations the view of man, and of man in the universe, in which every human life is sacred and the moral fruitfulness of its occurrence fostered and protected by us all.

What Is The Club of Life?

The international Club of Life was founded on October 20-22, 1982 in Rome at the initiative of Helga Zepp-LaRouche. Parallel founding conferences took place at that time in nine other cities on three continents. Over 1,300 scientists, physicians, teachers, and members of religious, civil rights, and human rights organizations from Africa, Ibero-America, Asia, North America, and Western Europe were represented at these conferences. As founding members, they committed themselves to organize for a solution to the world economic crisis through a new, just world economic order, and thereby to prevent mankind from descending into a new Dark Age.

Since this first series of international conferences, the membership of the Club of Life has quickly expanded. Active national chapters already exist in the Federal Republic of Germany, France, Italy, Spain, Sweden, Denmark, the United States, Mexico, and India. Preparations are under way for official founding conferences in Zaire, Nigeria, and Japan.

The founding of the Club of Life is a declaration of war against the Club of Rome, which is responsible for the neo-Malthusian fraud of alleged "limited resources, and against all those institutions which promote this inhuman doctrine of zero growth--whether in the guise 'of advocates of "population reduction," death with dignity, a cult of nature, or a "post-industrial society."

The Club of Life stands for the protection of human life and the value of the human being around the world,

There Are No Limits to Growth

wherever they are threatened by the economic and spiritual crises of our time. The Club of Life thus concerns itself with all important areas of activity, from economic and monetary policy and the theory and practice of scientific and technological progress, to the sphere of pedagogy, art, and culture.

The Club of Life
Founding Principles

WE THE UNDERSIGNED, declare:

1. Never before has the existence of human society been more threatened than today. The danger of global nuclear war as well as regional wars in the developing sector potentially threatens life on all continents of this earth.

2. A new world economic crisis and the effects of an unjust world economic order have massively increased hunger, epidemics, social chaos and regional wars throughout the world, particularly in the developing countries, and threaten the physical existence of more and more people.

3. Through the concurrence of a new world economic crisis and a growing potential cultural pessimism, there exists a great danger that the value of the life of the individual and the dignity of man should no longer be held inviolable. The brutality which de facto relegates whole groupings of men to the category of "useless eaters," whether they be old and sick people or people in the so-called "Third World," reveals the danger of a new fascism.

4. While the physical existence of mankind is threatened militarily, economically and morally, the "spiritual death" of a greater and greater portion of the population, particularly of the youth through drug addiction, constitutes an evil of the first order, which places in question the reproduction of the

humanity of the human species, since an unacceptably large part of the next generation is spiritually destroyed.

WE, THE UNDERSIGNED, therefore agree to the following principles:

1. The inalienable right to life for all the peoples of our planet must be defended. This means not only averting the danger of a global, thermonuclear war, as well as regional wars in the developing-sector countries, but also averting the dangers and conflicts, caused by Malthusian policies, which arise from a lack of economic development, and therewith finally eradicating war as the means of carrying out conflicts between states.

2. Human society has reached the point where only a just new world economic order can secure peace. The absolute sovereignty of nations, their absolute political and economic self-determination and the safeguarding of their legal equality by international treaties must be guaranteed. The legitimate pursuit of national interest should not contradict the interest of the world's population, but must contribute to an order of international cooperation which promotes the interest of all for freer, more sovereign development.

3. We require the renaissance of a new, worldwide humanism, based upon the principles of Judeo-Christian humanism and their reflections in the cultures of Asia and Africa, as well as upon the moral obligation to a new, just world economic order, for only thus can the inviolability of the life of the individual once again become self-evident. Human life must be defended from the time of

What is the Club of Life?

conception up to the time of death. These principles are embodied in the Book of Genesis, which commands: "Be fruitful, multiply, fill the Earth and subdue it." We reject the ideas of Malthusianism and their modern worshipers as evil and unscientific. The belief that today we can solve some of the most pressing problems in the world, the economic crisis and underdevelopment, through technological development goes hand in hand with the belief in the perfectibility of man. Only man's stress on his own spiritual nature, the cultivation of the gift of reason in all men, can create an atmosphere of cultural optimism, in which the highest good of man--life itself--is held inviolable.

October 22, 1982
Wiesbaden
West Germany

A Club of Life commission is reviewing further suggestions for an extension of these principles.

Lyndon H. LaRouche, Jr.

Biography of Lyndon H. LaRouche, Jr.

Lyndon H. LaRouche, Jr. was born in 1922 in Rochester, New Hampshire. After serving in the armed forces in the China-Burma-India theater during World War II, he ended his university studies and worked from 1947 to the mid-1960s as a management consultant. Since 1952, LaRouche has carried out intensive researches into the mathematical physics of Bernhard Riemann and Georg Cantor, which served as the basis for his later successes in the sphere of economic science.

In 1974, LaRouche founded an international news agency which publishes the political newsweekly *Executive Intelligence Review*. Since October 1979, *EIR* has issued regular quarterly economic forecasts which have proven themselves the only competent ones among all government and private econometrics services.

LaRouche is active in the National Democratic Policy Committee (NDPC) within the U.S. Democratic Party. In 1980 he ran for the Democratic presidential nomination on the platform of a program for overcoming the economic crisis, in the tradition of the "American System" of Alexander Hamilton.

In August 1983, LaRouche circulated his "Operation Juarez" proposal. This program, which has gained broad attention throughout Latin America, opened the way to orderly renegotiation of debts and recommended the creation of a Latin American "Common Market." These proposals formed the unofficial agenda of discussion at the summit meeting of the Andean Pact nations in the summer of 1983 and many other Latin American conferences.

In October 1982, Lyndon LaRouche and in particular his wife Helga Zepp-LaRouche initiated the Club Of Life, in order to build a counterpole to the anti-human ideology of the *Club of Rome*.

The NDPC currently has over 30,000 members and 300,000 supporters in the United States, and is backing 2,500 candidates at the local, regional, and national level. LaRouche's campaign organization for the 1984 Democratic presidential nomination, The LaRouche Campaign, is organizing a broad movement behind him. The editors of the *Executive Intelligence Review* published a biography of LaRouche in July 1983 under the title *Will This Man Become President?* The focal points of LaRouche's policy are his support for the development of defensive energy-beam weapons and his battle for a new world economic order on the basis of the most modern technology, centered on giant agro-industrial projects.

Since October 1979, LaRouche has publicly advocated the development of beam weapons, since only with the help of this technology, which can annihilate enemy missiles in flight, can the dangerous defense doctrine of "Mutually Assured Destruction" be superseded. In February 1982, LaRouche spoke on this subject at an EIR seminar in Washington, D.C., attended by leading Americans and Soviets. In March 1983, President Ronald Reagan announced that the development and deployment of space-based defensive beam weapons was now the official policy of the United States.

In July 1983 the LaRouches made a three-week trip to India, Thailand, and Japan, in order to better acquaint themselves with Asia's development potential. In collaboration with the Fusion Energy Foundation, LaRouche proposed five Great Projects which could make Asia into the center of world development: construction of a north-south canal in China, development of the Mekong

River, a canal across the Isthmus of Kra in Thailand, the Ganges-Brahmaputra irrigation project in India, and construction of a second Panama Canal. These development projects would not only make this region, with its 2.5 billion people, into the largest construction site in the world, but would serve as the motor for overcoming the global economic depression.

Made in the USA
Columbia, SC
01 August 2019